Catholic Faith Teaching Manual

Level 3 : Intermediary Level

Learn the Heart of God from the Word of God

Pope Saint Gregory the Great

Copyright © 2021 by Father Raymond Taouk. All rights reserved.

"No part of this publication may be reproduced, distributed, or transmitted in any form or by any means, including photocopying, recording, or other electronic or mechanical methods, or by any information storage and retrieval system without the prior written permission of the publisher, except in the case of very brief quotations embodied in critical reviews and certain other noncommercial uses permitted by copyright law."

Co published with JMJ Catholic products.
www.jmjcatholicproducts.com.au
Email : jeanette@jmjcatholicproducts.com.au

ISBN: 9780645021929

TABLE OF CONTENTS

		Page
Lesson 1	Catechism : The Redemption	
	Questions : 46, 47, 48, 49	9
	Prayer : Definition	10
	Bible Story : The Israelites enter the Promised Land	11
	The Saints : Saint Scholastica	12
	Devotions : Stations of the Cross	14
	The First Station : Jesus us condemned to death	15
	General : Hymns	16
Lesson 2	Catechism : The Redemption	
	Questions 50, 51, 52	20
	Prayer : The three Hail Marys	22
	Bible Story : Samuel	23
	The Saints : Saint Ignatius of Loyola	24
	The Second Station : Jesus is made to carry His cross	26
	General : Our Guardian Angel	27
Lesson 3	Catechism : The Holy Ghost and Grace	
	Questions 53, 54, 55	30
	Prayer : Spiritual Communion	31
	Bible Story : David	32
	The Saints : Saint George	34
	The Third Station : Jesus falls the first time	36
	General : Sacramentals	37
Lesson 4	Catechism : The Holy Ghost and Grace	
	Questions 56, 57, 58	40
	Prayer : The Lords Prayer	41
	Bible Story : David and Goliath	42
	The Saints : Saint Gregory the Great	44

		Page
Lesson 4	The Fourth Station : Jesus meets His sorrowful mother	46
	General : The Altar	48
Lesson 5	Catechism : The Virtues and Gifts of the Holy Ghost	
	Questions 59, 60, 61	52
	Prayer : Prayer for Gaining Indulgences	53
	Bible : Solomon	54
	The Saints : Saint Aloysius Gonzaga	55
	The Fifth Station : Simon of Cyrene helps Jesus.	56
	General : The Sacred Vestments	57
	General : Vestment colors	58
Lesson 6	Catechism : The Virtues and Gifts of the Holy Ghost	
	Questions 62, 63, 64	62
	Prayer : Examination of Conscience	63
	Prayer : The Commandments of the Church	65
	Bible Story : The division of the Kingdom	66
	The Saints : Saint Catherine of Alexandria	67
	The Sixth Station : Veronica wipes the face of Jesus	68
	General : Our Sunday Best	69
Lesson 7	Catechism : The Catholic Church	
	Questions 65, 66, 67, 68	72
	Prayer : Prayer to our Patron Saint	73
	Bible Story : Jesus blesses the little children	74
	The Saints : Saint Francis Xavier	76
	The Seventh Station : Jesus falls the second time	78
	The Spiritual Work of Mercy	79
Lesson 8	Catechism : The Catholic Church	
	Questions : 69, 70, 71	82
	Prayer : Memorare	83
	Bible Story : Jesus walks on water	84

		Page
Lesson 8	The Saints : Saint Nicholas De Flue	86
	The Eight Station : The women of Jerusalem weep over Jesus	88
Lesson 9	Catechism : The Marks of the Church	
	Questions 72, 73, 74, 75	92
	Prayer : Act of Faith, Hope and Charity	93
	Bible Story : The blind man	94
	The Saints : Saint Jane Frances De Chantal	95
	The Ninth Station : Jesus falls the third time	96
	The 2nd Spiritual Work of Mercy	97
Lesson 10	Catechism : The Communion of Saints and Forgiveness of sins	
	Questions 76, 77	100
	Prayer : Prayer for the Pope	101
	Bible Story : The Good Samaritan	102
	The Saints : Saint Bridget of Sweden	104
	The Tenth Station : Jesus is stripped of His garment	106
	The 3rd Spiritual Work of Mercy	107
Lesson 11	Catechism : The Resurrection and Life Everlasting	
	Questions 78, 79, 80	110
	Prayer : Prayer for the Conversion of Australia	111
	Bible Story : The Lost Sheep	112
	The Saints : Saint Margaret Mary	114
	The Eleventh Station : Jesus is nailed to the cross	116
	The 4th Spiritual Work of Mercy	117
Lesson 12	Catechism : The Resurrection and Life Everlasting	
	Questions 81, 82, 83	120
	Prayer : Aspirations	121
	Bible Story : The Prodigal Son	122
	The Saints : Saint Martin of Tours	124
	The Twelfth Station : Jesus is nailed to the cross	126

		Page
Lesson 12	The 5th Spiritual Work of Mercy	127
Lesson 13	Catechism : The Two Great Commandments	
	Questions 84, 85, 86	130
	Prayer : Hail Holy Queen	131
	Bible Story : The rich man and Lazarus	132
	The Saints : Saint Terese of Avila	133
	The Thirteenth Station : Jesus is taken down	134
	The 5th Spiritual Work of Mercy	135
Lesson 14	Catechism : The Ten Commandments	
	Questions 87	138
	Prayer : Anima Christi	139
	Bible Story : Jesus raises Lazarus from the dead	140
	The Saints : Saint Louis IX	142
	The Fourteenth Station of the Cross	144
	The 6th Spiritual Work of Mercy	145
Lesson 15	Catechism Questions 46 - 51	148
	Catechism Questions 52 - 60	149
	Catechism Questions 61-69	150
	Catechism Questions 70 - 79	151
	Catechism Questions 80 - 86	152
	Catechism Questions 87	153

Lesson 1

Level 3

Intermediary Level

Level 3 - Lesson 1

Catechism

Each lesson we are going to study some catechism questions. This is the most important part of your lesson. These questions you must learn by heart so that you will come to know a great deal about God and His wonderful creation. Level Two studied forty five catechism questions, so we commence this Level with Catechism Question 46.

May God bless you in your study of Himself and His holy Church.

The Redemption

46. **What is meant by the Redemption?**
By the Redemption is meant that Jesus Christ offered His sufferings and death to God in satisfaction for the sins of men.

47. **What do we learn from the sufferings and death of Christ?**
From the sufferings and death of Christ we learn God's love for man and the evil of sin.

48. **What do we mean when we say in the Apostles' Creed that Christ descended into hell?**
When we say that Christ descended into hell, we mean that after He died, the soul of Christ descended into a place or state of rest, called limbo, where the souls of the just were waiting for Him.

49. **When did Christ rise from the dead?**
Christ rose from the dead, glorious and immortal, on Easter Sunday, the third day after His death.

After the sin of Adam and Eve (Original Sin), death entered the world. God made us for heaven, but through our first parents we rejected Him by choosing sin over Him. God so loved man that He promised to send a Saviour – His own Son to redeem us. So thousands of years later, Jesus came to the Earth as a man, and died on the Cross for us. He redeemed us, but He wants us to correspond with His graces that we might one day be saved and be with Him forever in Heaven. Through the redemption therefore, the gates of Heaven have been opened, all we need to do is God's Will, and we will one day walk through those sacred gates and be with God forever.

Question 1 ❖ What is meant by the Redemption?

Question 2 ❖ What do we learn from the sufferings and death of Christ?

Question 3 ❖ When did Christ rise from the dead?

Prayer

Usually, a new prayer is learned each lesson, but to commence our studies this year, we are going to look at what prayer is. This is most important to understand. When new prayers are taught in this level, it is not sufficient just to learn the prayers, but to pray them. Many of the prayers you may know already and others will be new to you. Let us learn the definition of prayer. This needs to be learned by heart and understood.

Definition : Prayer is the lifting up of the heart and mind to God in Adoration, Thanksgiving, Reparation and Petition.

Adoration is bowing to God as our Supreme Creator and acknowledging that we are mere creatures.
Thanksgiving means that we must thank God for everything He has given us.
Reparation means making up for our sins and the sins of others.
Petition is asking God for all the things we need to love Him and one day to get to Heaven – our true home.

When we talk to God, we can use our own words or we can use some beautiful and meaningful words written by others. There are five main sources of spoken prayers:

- Our own made up prayers
- Prayers Given to us by Our Lord Himself e.g. The Lord's Prayer
- Biblical passages; the inspired word of God e.g. The Hail Mary
- Prayers Composed by the Saints e.g. Saint Bernard's Memorare
- Prayers Composed by the Church e.g. The Acts of Faith, Hope and Charity

Remember, prayers are not only words, they are the raising of our minds and hearts to God.

Question 4   ❖   Write out the definition of prayer

Question 5   ❖   List any three of the main sources of spoken prayers

Level 3 - Lesson 1

Bible Story

Each lesson we are going to present a story from the Bible. It may come from the Old Testament (before Jesus was born) or from the New Testament (after Jesus was born). Stories from the Bible are very important for us because God Himself, through the Sacred Authors, wrote the Bible, so everything we read in the Bible is absolutely true.

The Israelites Enter the Promised Land

After the death of Moses, the Lord commanded Josue to lead the Israelites across the river Jordan into Chanaan. On the banks of the river, the same miracle that had taken place at the passage of the Red Sea was repeated, for the water rolled back, leaving a dry passage. When the Israelites had crossed over they camped near Jericho, where they celebrated the feast of the Pasch. This feast was kept every year in memory of their release from Egypt. Jericho was a large city surrounded by strong walls. God commanded the Israelites to march around the city for seven days. They carried with them the Ark of the Covenant, a box made of most precious wood covered inside and out with gold, in which were kept the two tablets of the Law (the Ten Commandments). For the first six days they carried the Ark one circuit. On the seventh day, after they had gone around seven times, they sounded the trumpets of jubilee. At the sound of these trumpets and the shouts of the people, the walls fell in and the Israelites entered and took the city. In time, Josue conquered all the country, and so after long wandering, the Israelites settled in the Promised Land.

Question 6 ❖ What was the name of the feast the Israelites celebrated each year in memory of their release from Egypt?

Question 7 ❖ What was carried in the Ark of the Covenant?

The Saints

Saint Scholastica

Saint Benedict was the first of the holy monks. Saint Scholastica was his beloved sister. He built monasteries for holy men. She built convents for holy women. Saint Benedict loved his sister very much.

In their days there was much evil and the world was full of dangers for good women. Bands of wicked soldiers roamed all over the world. So Saint Scholastica built beautiful convents that were peaceful for a place where women can stay and be safe.

One day Saint Benedict sat and talked with his sister about God. Night came and he said, "I must go back to my home." "Please don't go," she said. For she knew she was going to die. When her brother, Saint Benedict, insisted upon leaving, she bowed her head and prayed. Suddenly a great storm burst. The wind blew. The rain fell. The lightning flashed. Saint Benedict could not go back. So all night long they sang together, they prayed together, they talked about God.

Three days later, Saint Scholastica died and Saint Benedict saw her soul going up to heaven in the form of a pure, white dove.

Saint Scholastica's feast day is February 10th.

Question 8 ❖ Who was Saint Scholastica's brother?

Question 9 ❖ What good work did Saint Scholastica do for women?

Question 10 ❖ Relate in your own words what happened on the night, three days before Saint Scholastica died.

Devotions

Stations of the Cross

The Stations of the Cross, or The Way of the Cross as it is sometimes called is the most heavily indulgenced devotion in the Catholic Church. It is to be the topic of our lessons this year. All the Saints have encouraged us to meditate upon Our Lord's passion and death, and the Stations of the Cross do just that; from the unjust condemnation of Pilate to the laying of Our Lord's body in the Holy Sepulchre (tomb).

All Catholic churches have set up the fourteen Stations of the Cross, whether they be paintings, plaster molds, copper relief or even small plain crosses. The faithful are encouraged to go from station to station meditating upon Our Lord's sacred passion. So important does the Church consider this devotion, that it has attached a plenary indulgence to this act. Over the year, in our lessons, we will be meditating upon each Station and let us ask us dear Lord, as we study His passion, to love Him more and more, and to imitate Him as best we can.

Question 11 ❖ How many Stations of the Cross are there?

Question 12 ❖ List three ways the Stations of the Cross may be presented in a church.

Level 3 - Lesson 1

The First Station

Jesus is Condemned to Death

Jesus was brought before Pontius Pilate, the Governor of Judea, and on at least three occasions, Pilate said he found no guilt in Jesus, and yet, through the pressure of the Jewish priests and the people, he had Our Lord scourged and then sentenced to death.

Pilate, trying to show that he didn't want to condemn Our Lord to the Cross said, "I wash my hands of the blood of this innocent man" but in the same breath, he said to the people, Take him yourselves and crucify him, for I find no guilt in him. He allowed them to crucify Jesus, having his own Roman soldiers carry out the greatest crime in the history of the world; that of crucifying God.

When we meditate upon this mystery, we ask Our dear Lord to help us when we are unjustly treated, to offer it up in reparation for our sins.

Question 13

Who condemned Jesus to death?

Question 14

Write out the first Station of the Cross.

Question 15

What was so unjust (unfair) about what Pilate did?

General

Hymns

People do a lot of talking! When we go to school, the teacher and children talk. At home we talk a lot with our family. Our day is made up of much talking. Sometimes when we talk, we speak of happy things, at other times, sad things.

God has given us voices and it is therefore a good thing to do, that is, to talk. We must control our talking and we must never talk badly of someone. Most of all we should use our tongues to talk of our dear Lord and God. What a wonderful way to use the voice God has given us.

Well, we can also sing. Some of us like singing very much and others, perhaps not so much. Like when we talk, we should sing good things, and what pleases God most is when we sing about Him or His holy Mother or of the angels and saints.

Saint Augustine (a great Saint who was very learned) once said, "When we sing, we pray twice". Yes, that is right. If we sing to God, praising Him, thanking Him, telling Him we are sorry or even asking Him for things, we are praying twice and gaining double the merit. What an easy thing to do!

When we sing songs about God, His holy Mother or His angels and saints, we call these holy songs, Hymns. The most common time for singing hymns is before and after Mass or during processions of the Blessed Sacrament. But we can sing hymns at almost any time and any place. Perhaps you could ask your parents if you could sing some hymns at home, perhaps every Sunday, or holy day. There are many places where you can praise God with your singing.

Some of you may say, "I have a terrible voice; God wouldn't want to hear me singing". Well, God does not so much listen to the tone of your voice when you sing, but He listens to the sentiments of your heart. The singing of hymns is a good and holy thing to do.

Question 16 ❖ What did Saint Augustine say about singing?

Question 17 ❖ What is a hymn?

Lesson 2

Level 3

Intermediary Level

Catechism

The Redemption

50. When did Christ ascend into heaven?

Christ ascended, body and soul, into heaven on Ascension Day, forty days after His Resurrection.

51. What do we mean when we say that Christ sits at the right hand of God, the Father Almighty?

When we say that Christ sits at the right hand of God, the Father Almighty, we mean that Our Lord as God is equal to the Father, and that as man He has the highest place in heaven, next to God.

52. What do we mean when we say that Christ will come from thence to judge the living and the dead?

When we say that Christ will come from thence to judge the living and the dead, we mean that on the last day Our Lord will come to judge everyone who has ever lived in this world.

The three catechism questions this week require much learning and understanding, particularly questions 51 and 52. The three persons of the Blessed Trinity are equal. Therefore Jesus, the second Person of the Trinity is equal to His Father. This is strange to us, as our earthly fathers are our superiors, but not so with God. The three sacred Persons of the Blessed Trinity are equal with each other.

At the end of the world, the second Person of the Blessed Trinity, Jesus Himself, will come back to our world to judge all people from all times. It will be called The General Judgment. Thus we must live good and sinless lives here on the Earth, so that our judgment will be a favorable one.

Question 1 ❖ When did Christ ascend into heaven?

Question 2 ❖ What is meant by the Redemption?

Question 3 ❖ When did Christ rise from the dead?

Prayer

The Three Hail Marys

We have by now already learned the Hail Mary. Along with the Our Father and the Glory Be, it is probably the most frequent prayer we pray. We include it here as a revision, as it is necessary for the devotion, The Three Hail Marys.

Hail Mary, full of grace, the Lord is with you, Blessed are you amongst women and blessed is the fruit of your womb, Jesus. Holy Mary, Mother of God, pray for us sinners, now and at the hour of our death. Amen

Our Lady at Fatima said that more souls go to hell because of sins against purity than any other sin. It makes sense then, to protect ourselves against sins of impurity by calling upon our most immaculate Blessed Mother to help us to be pure. The devotion of the Three Hail Marys is a wonderful and easy way to invoke Our Lady's help.

Method of Prayer: Hail Mary….

By thy Immaculate Conception O Mary, make my body pure and my soul holy. My Mother, preserve me this day (night) from mortal sin.

The Hail Mary and this prayer are repeated three times.

The Three Hail Marys can be said at any time of the day, but perhaps the best time would be during Morning and/or Night Prayers. The best way to learn this prayer is by saying it every day before the Lesson. That way, you will both learn it and please God by saying this prayer every day and it will start you on the way to learning a very good habit.

Question 4   ❖   When is the best time to pray the Three Hail Marys?

Question 5   ❖   Write out the part of the Three Hail Marys devotion beginning with the words, By thy Immaculate Conception…

Question 6   ❖   Write out the definition of prayer

Level 2 - Lesson 2

Bible Story

Samuel

When slavery had taught the Israelites sorrow for their sins, God sent great men, called judges, to set them free and to rule them. The last of these judges was named Samuel. His parents were very pious people, who for a long while had no children. They prayed to God to send them a son, and just as He listened to the prayer of Elizabeth, eleven hundred years afterward, so He heard their prayer and gave them Samuel. When the little boy was three years old, his mother took him to Heli the high-priest, and consecrated him to God. One night when Samuel was sleeping in the temple, the Lord called him. The boy thought it was Heli, and ran to him, but the priest said: "I did not call you, my son; go back and sleep." The call was repeated three times, so Samuel knew it was the Lord, and cried out, "Speak, Lord, for I am your servant." Then the Lord told him that He will punish Heli and his two sons; the father, because he was too easy with his sons and had not punished them for their wickedness, and the sons because they offended Him by many sins. Some time after, the sons were killed in battle, and when Heli heard the sad news, he fell backward and broke his neck.

Samuel succeeded Heli as judge, and ruled wisely and well, but when he grew old he appointed his sons judges over Israel. The sons were not like their father; they did not fear God, and the people became dissatisfied, and asked for a king. This did not please Samuel, because he wished that God alone should be king of Israel. But the Lord told him do as the people wanted, so he anointed, as their king, Saul, a beautiful and brave youth of the tribe of Benjamin. At first God was with Saul, and gave him the victory over his enemies, but later Saul disobeyed God, and he was cut off from the throne of Israel.

Question 7 ❖ Who did Samuel appoint as the king of Israel?

Question 8 ❖ What did Samuel say to the Lord at the age of three after the Lord had called him three times?

Question 9 ❖ What was carried in the Ark of the Covenant?

The Saints

Saint Ignatius of Loyola

There are two great saints named Ignatius. One was the bishop of Antioch. Saint John the Apostle taught him to know and love Jesus. The other saint who is the subject of this lesson was a brave soldier and is called Saint Ignatius of Loyola.

One day he was wounded badly in battle. When he was getting well, he read the Lives of the Saints. "What they did, I can do!" he thought. And so he became a brave soldier of Christ. He established a new Society of priests and brothers. He called it the Society of Jesus (Jesuits). Among other great things he did, he also established in the world what we know today as the Ignatian Retreats. (a retreat of thirty days where the priests/brothers renew their allegiance to Christ their King – this retreat has been shortened to five days for the faithful).

The feast of Saint Ignatius is July 31st.

Question 10 ❖ What was the name of the Society started by Saint Ignatius of Loyola?

Question 11 ❖ What great work did Saint Ignatius establish in the world?

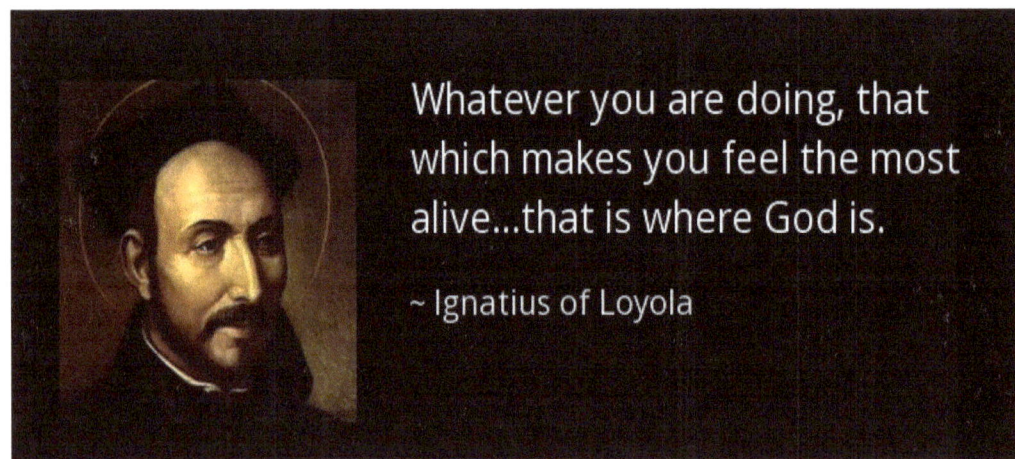

The Second Station

Jesus is made to Carry His Cross

After being found innocent by Pilate, and yet sentenced to death Jesus was given a rough, wooden cross made by the Roman executioners. This heavy cross was thrust upon Our Lord's sacred shoulders that had already been scourged.

Our Lord accepted this Cross without one word of complaint. He was carrying the Cross for us – for our sins. Every time we commit a sin, we are adding more weight to this Cross that Jesus so lovingly carried for us.

When we meditate upon this station, let us promise Jesus that we will offer up all the little crosses He sends us in reparation for our sins.

Question 12 ❖ Who made the wooden Cross that Jesus had to carry?

Question 13 ❖ How did Our Lord accept the Cross that was given to Him?

Question 14 ❖ Who condemned Jesus to death?

Question 15 ❖ Write out the first Station of the Cross.

Level 2 - Lesson 2

General

Our Guardian Angel

From the moment we are born, God sends us a helper; our very own Angel. He is given to us to guard us from harm, to protect us from dangers, physical and spiritual, to guide us to do good and to lead us to heaven. He is our special friend, our Guardian Angel. Everybody ever born is given a Guardian Angel; it is even said that priests are given two Guardian Angels. God must love us so much to give us this wonderful friend who is with us all our lives. He whispers good inspirations (thoughts) into our ears and is always there if we need him. It is sad that many people do not even know they have a Guardian Angel. It is more sad that many people who know they have a Guardian Angel never even listen to him.

In Level One we learnt a Prayer to our Guardian Angel. This is not just a prayer for children; it is a prayer for all Catholics, young and old. If we have forgotten to pray to our special angel, make today the day to start praying to him again. He is waiting for us to ask him. So let us be very good friends with our guardian angel, let us run to him when we need help and let us seek his protection from the devil.

Question 16 ❖ Who is the special friend that God gives to all people to help them throughout their lives?

Question 17 ❖ Write out the prayer to your Guardian Angel (from Level One)

Question 18 ❖ What did Saint Augustine say about singing?

Lesson 3

Level 3

Post Communion Level

Catechism

The Holy Ghost & Grace

53. **Who is the Holy Ghost?**

The Holy Ghost is God and the third Person of the Blessed Trinity.

54. **What does the Holy Ghost do for the salvation of mankind?**

The Holy Ghost sanctifies souls through the gift of grace.

55. **How many kinds of grace are there?**

There are two kinds of grace: sanctifying grace and actual grace.

In this lesson we begin our study of Grace. The Holy Ghost, the third Person of the Blessed Trinity was sent by the Father and the Son on Pentecost Sunday. What a day of Grace for the world. It was the birth day of the Church. Through the Holy Ghost we receive God's wonderful gift of grace. It is this gift of grace that we need if we are to win heaven one day. We should always pray to the Holy Ghost that He shower us with grace that we may be more pleasing to God.

In future lessons we will study the two types of grace; sanctifying grace and actual grace. This topic of grace is a very important one. Let us pray to Saint Augustine (sometimes called the Doctor of Grace because of his wonderful writings on the subject) to help us understand better the mysteries of grace.

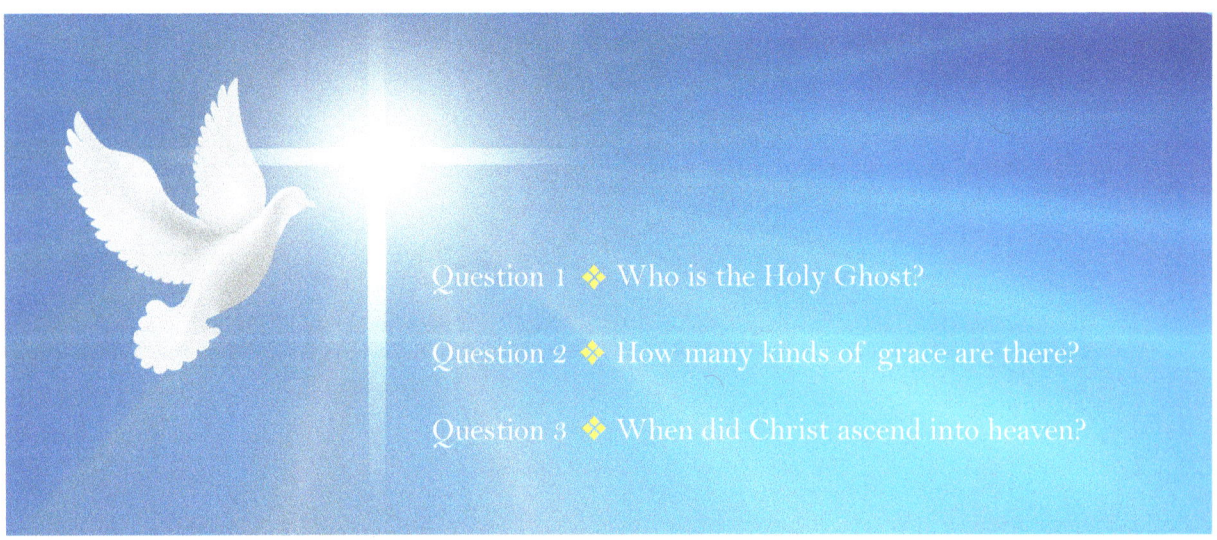

Question 1 ❖ Who is the Holy Ghost?

Question 2 ❖ How many kinds of grace are there?

Question 3 ❖ When did Christ ascend into heaven?

Level 3 - Lesson 3

Prayer

Spiritual Communion

For one reason or another, we cannot always receive Our Lord in the Blessed Sacrament. It is possible, however, to receive Him spiritually, indeed, many times a day. Saying this prayer is very pleasing to God as it shows our love for Him, and it shows that we desire to be near Him throughout our day. If you have the opportunity to visit the Blessed Sacrament, this prayer is an ideal one to say.

Question 4 ❖ When is a good time to make a Spiritual Communion?

Question 5 ❖ Write out the Spiritual Communion.

Question 6 ❖ Write out the part of the Three Hail Marys devotion beginning with the words, By thy Immaculate Conception...

Bible Story

David

At the command of God, Samuel went to Bethlehem, to the house of Isai, whose youngest son, David, was chosen by God to replace Saul. David, was tending his father's flocks, when Samuel arrived. Samuel sent for him David and anointed him.

At that moment the Spirit of the Lord departed from Saul and he became sad. Saul ordered his servants to find someone who could play the harp and cheer him with its music. One of the servants told him of David, who was a skillful player, so Saul sent for him, and was so much pleased with David's playing that he made him his armour-bearer.

Question 7 ❖ How did David cheer up Saul?

Question 8 ❖ Who did Samuel appoint as the king of Israel?

Question 9 ❖ Who anointed David?

The Saints

Saint George

George was a Roman soldier a long time ago. Most people then did not know Our Lord or love Him. But George's parents did. George became a soldier because he was brave and strong. Now the wicked Roman Emperor (Diocletian) began to kill the Christians. He ordered his soldiers to arrest and kill them too. George refused to do this. Instead, he told the Emperor that everyone should believe in Jesus Christ and follow him.

The Emperor was furious and threw the young soldier into prison. He was tortured and killed. George was happy to die and be a Martyr for Christ. Soldiers always remember and love young Colonel George. They know he hated evil and fought it. The soldiers would sing songs about Saint George and how he slew the great dragon of sin, evil and cowardice.

Saint George is the patron of all brave men. He is the favorite Patron of England.

The feast of Saint George is April 23rd.

Question 10 ❖ What was the name of the Roman Emperor who ordered the killing of the Christians and whom Saint George refused to obey?

Question 11 ❖ Which country has as its favorite Saint (patron saint) George?

Question 12 ❖ Saint George is the patron of who?

Question 12 ❖ What do we mean when we say Saint George was a Martyr for Christ?

Question 14 ❖ What was the name of the Society started by Saint Ignatius of Loyola?

The Third Station

Jesus Falls the First Time

Jesus was so weakened by His scourging, His crowning with thorns, His agony in the Garden and His other sufferings, that He fell under the weight of the Cross. What weighed down His Cross so much? It was our sins. Every time we sin we add a little more to the sufferings of our dear Saviour.

This Station is also a reminder to us that after we have fallen by our sins, we must rise up and tell God we are sorry, and promise Him that we will try never to sin again.

Jesus fell, not because of His own sins (as He is sinless) but on account of our sins. Let us promise Our Lord that we will accept the crosses He gives us and that we will fight hard never to commit a deliberate sin.

Question 15 ❖ List the first three Stations of the Cross.

Question 16 ❖ Why did Jesus fall under the weight of the Cross?

Question 17 ❖ Who made the wooden Cross that Jesus had to carry?

Level 2 - Lesson 2

General

Sacramentals

Once an enemy handed a cup of poisoned wine to Saint John. When Saint John took the cup, he made the Sign of the Cross over it and then drank it. It did not hurt him at all. What caused this miracle? It was the power of the Sign of the Cross.

We call the Sign of the Cross a Sacramental. Sacramentals are holy actions like the Sign of the Cross, and holy things such as holy water, rosaries, medals, scapulars, crucifixes, statues, candles, palms, which the Church blesses for our use.

The chief kinds of Sacramentals are:

1. The blessings given by priests and bishops
2. The driving out from persons or things the evil spirits that possess them.
3. All blessed objects

The name sacramental has been given to them because they resemble the sacraments in that they are outward signs and a means of grace. The sacraments were instituted by Christ and give grace of themselves. The sacramentals, on the other hand, were instituted by the Church, but they of themselves do not give grace. If we use them with faith and devotion, they will obtain for us an increase of grace. The Church can add new sacramentals or change sacramentals that already exist, but no person on earth can change the number of sacraments.

The sacramentals obtain for us many benefits which are:

1. Actual graces
2. The forgiveness of venial sins
3. The remission of temporal punishment
4. Health of body and material blessings
5. Protection from evil spirits.

The greater the devotion we have and the more fervent the prayers which the sacramentals arouse in us, the greater are the benefits we derive from them.

Question 18 ❖ How many chief kinds of Sacramentals are there?

Question 19 ❖ List two differences between a Sacrament and a Sacramental?

Question 20 ❖ List three different Sacramentals

Question 21 ❖ Who is the special friend that God gives to all people to help them throughout their lives?

Lesson 4

Level 3

Post Communion Level

Catechism

The Holy Ghost & Grace

56. **What does sanctifying grace do for us?**

Sanctifying grace:
first, makes us holy and pleasing to God;
second, makes us adopted children of God;
third, makes us temples of the Holy Ghost;
fourth, gives us the right to heaven.

57. **What is actual grace?**

Actual grace is a supernatural help from God which enlightens our mind and strengthens our will to do good and to avoid evil.

58. **What are the principal ways of obtaining grace?**

The principal ways of obtaining grace are prayer and the sacraments, especially the Holy Eucharist.

The two types of Grace are Sanctifying Grace and Actual Grace. Actual Grace is that grace which we receive throughout the day; the inspirations we receive to do good and to avoid evil. After we commit a sin (disobedience to God's law) we receive an actual grace from God that we might tell Him we are sorry for our sins. Yes, we need a grace to even be sorry for our sins.

Sanctifying Grace is the Life of God in us. It is this grace that we so despise when we commit Mortal Sin. When we choose to disobey God in a serious way by committing Mortal Sin, we lose Sanctifying Grace; we tell God to leave our souls! All we have to do on this Earth is to stay in the state of Sanctifying Grace, and we will be pleasing to Our Lord and we will merit Heaven.

Question 1 ❖ What does sanctifying grace do for us?

Question 2 ❖ What are the principal ways of obtaining grace?

Question 3 ❖ How many kinds of grace are there?

Level 3 - Lesson 4

Prayer

The Lord's Prayer

Our Father, Who art in heaven, hallowed be Thy Name. Thy Kingdom come, Thy Will be done on earth as it is in heaven. Give us this day our daily bread and forgive us our trespasses as we forgive those who trespass against us and lead us not into temptation, but deliver us from evil. Amen.

We learnt the Lord's Prayer (the Our Father) in Level One, but it is such an important prayer that is well worth revising it here. It was the Apostles who went to Our Blessed Lord and asked Him to teach them how to pray. It was then, that He taught them this most beautiful prayer.
It is important to understand what we are praying about when we say the Our Father; this prayer we pray so often. We divide the prayer up into two main sections. The first part is a prayer of praise. We are praying that God's Kingdom be not only in heaven, but on earth. We are praying that all creatures adore God as their King (Oh, if only the world today treated God as their King!). The second part of the prayer is that of petition. We are asking God to look after us, to give us our needs, spiritual and temporal. Most importantly, we are asking God to protect us from the devil and temptation.

Next time you pray the Lord's Prayer, think about what you are praying

Question 4 ❖ Who made up the Lord's Prayer?

Question 5 ❖ What is another name for the Lord's Prayer?

Question 6 ❖ Why did Jesus teach us the Lord's Prayer?

Bible Story

David and Goliath

A war broke out between the Israelites and the Philistines their chief enemy, and as the three eldest sons of Isai were in the army with Saul, David returned home to his father. When the two armies were drawn up opposite each other, a terrible giant, named Goliath, came forth from the Philistine camp, and dared any of the Israelites to fight him hand to hand. Although Saul was a great warrior, he and his entire army were frightened at this, and none of them dared meet Goliath. For forty days the giant repeated his challenge. At the end of that time David came to the camp to see his brothers. He saw Goliath, heard his words and was grieved that no one had the courage to fight him. Going to Saul, David said: "I will fight this Philistine." At first the king would not let him attempt it, but as David insisted, the king gave him a suit of armor and a helmet of brass.

David was not used to such things, and he could not wear them; but, choosing five smooth stones out of the stream, and taking his sling in his hand he went ahead to meet the giant.

Goliath seeing this fair young man come out to fight him, thought that he would have an easy victory, but when they came near to each other, David took one of the stones that he carried with him, put it into his sling and swung it rapidly round and round. The stone flew out and struck the giant on the forehead with such force that he fell to the ground. David ran up, drew the sword of Goliath from its sheath, and cut off his head.

When the Philistines saw this they were frightened and fled, and the Israelites following killed many of them. After Saul's death David was chosen King of Israel. He ruled for forty years, and when he died he left a great kingdom and a great name.

This victory of David over Goliath was a figure of Our Saviour's victory over the devil, for as David conquered Goliath with a staff and five smooth stones, so did our Blessed Lord conquer the devil by His Cross and His five wounds.

Question 7 ❖ From what camp did Goliath come?

Question 8 ❖ How did David kill Goliath?

Question 9 ❖ What did the victory of David over Goliath represent?

The Saints

Saint Gregory the Great

Young Gregory's father was very rich. When his father died, Gregory gave all the money he inherited to the poor. Then he went to a monastery and became a monk. He prayed. He studied hard. The Pope of those days heard about this bright young man. He called Gregory to Rome. He made him a Deacon. He sent him on important errands to kings and generals.

One day in the market place, Gregory saw some slaves. They told him they were Angles (members of the tribe named Angles). "You should be Angels," he said. English boys were called 'Angles' in those days. Gregory knew they did not believe in Jesus. You see, he hoped they would be Catholics.

When the Pope died, the people made Gregory the Pope. He remembered the English boys. So he sent Saint Augustine to England to tell them about Jesus and to make them Catholics. He sent holy priests to convert the Spanish and the French. Wicked men came rushing into Italy to destroy it. He told them about Jesus, and they became Catholics too.

He wrote great books which are still read today. He taught people how to sing in Church. We still call these songs the Gregorian Chants. He was one of the greatest Popes that ever lived.

Saint Gregory Feast day is March 12th.

Question 10 ❖ What position did Saint Gregory hold in the Church?

Question 11 ❖ Who did Saint Gregory send to England to tell them about Jesus and make them Catholics?

Question 12 ❖ After whom is Gregorian Chant (Church music) named?

Question 13 ❖ Which country has as its favorite saint (patron saint) Saint George?

The Fourth Station

Jesus Meets His Sorrowful Mother

This was perhaps the greatest suffering Our Lord had to endure on His way to Calvary. His eyes met the sorrowing eyes of His Mother Mary. Seeing the suffering of Our Blessed Lady, Our Lord's suffering was also increased. No greater love has Our Lord for any creature than the love He had for Mary. To see His Mother suffer so much on His account, increased His own sufferings.

When we meditate on this fourth Station of the Cross, let us not only comfort Jesus in His suffering by our prayers and sacrifices, but let us turn to Mary and be a comfort to her Sorrowful and Immaculate Heart.

What greater way can we show our love for God than by loving His holy Mother, by praying to her and by having great confidence in her intercession.

Question 14 ❖ What is the fourth Station of the Cross?

Question 15 ❖ Why was the meeting of Jesus and His Mother such a great sorrow for Our Lord?

Question 16 ❖ Who made the wooden Cross that Jesus had to carry?

General

The Altar

The priest must have an altar on which to offer the Holy Sacrifice of the Mass. He also needs sacred vessels and sacred vestments. The Altar of Sacrifice is the table on which the sacrifice is offered.

Altar Stone. In the middle of this table is a flat stone with a small hole in the center. In this hole rest the relics of some martyrs. This is the stone that the priest kisses when he kisses the altar.

Altar Cloths. Three white linens cover the altar. The top one reaches to the floor at the ends.

Antependium. In front of the altar hangs a cloth which is of the same color as that of the feast day. This cloth is called the Antependium. Some altars do not have an Antependium.

Altar Crucifix. There is a crucifix above the altar to remind us that the Holy Sacrifice of the Mass is the same as the Sacrifice of the Cross.

Tabernacle. On the altar is the tabernacle, which is Jesus' home on earth. Jesus is in the ciborium inside the tabernacle.

Sanctuary Lamp. Whenever Jesus is present in the tabernacle the red sanctuary lamp must burn day and night. It tells everyone who comes into the church that Jesus is there on the altar.

Candles. On either side of the tabernacle are three candles. Two candles must be lighted when Holy Mass is said. Six are lighted at High Mass.

Altar Cards. There are also three altar cards, on which are printed certain important Mass prayers.

Missal. The Missal is the large book which contains all the prayers of the Mass.

Altar Steps. The steps leading up to the altar remind the priest and us of the hill of Calvary.

Bell. The server rings a little bell at the principal parts of the Mass. The bell tells us to be alert and watch closely.

Level 3 - Lesson 4

General

Credence Table. Off to the side is a small table called the Credence Table. On it are the cruets, a glass bowl and a small linen towel for the priest to use when he washes his fingers.

Cruets. The cruets are the two small glass bottles. One cruet holds the wine, and the other holds the water for the sacrifice.

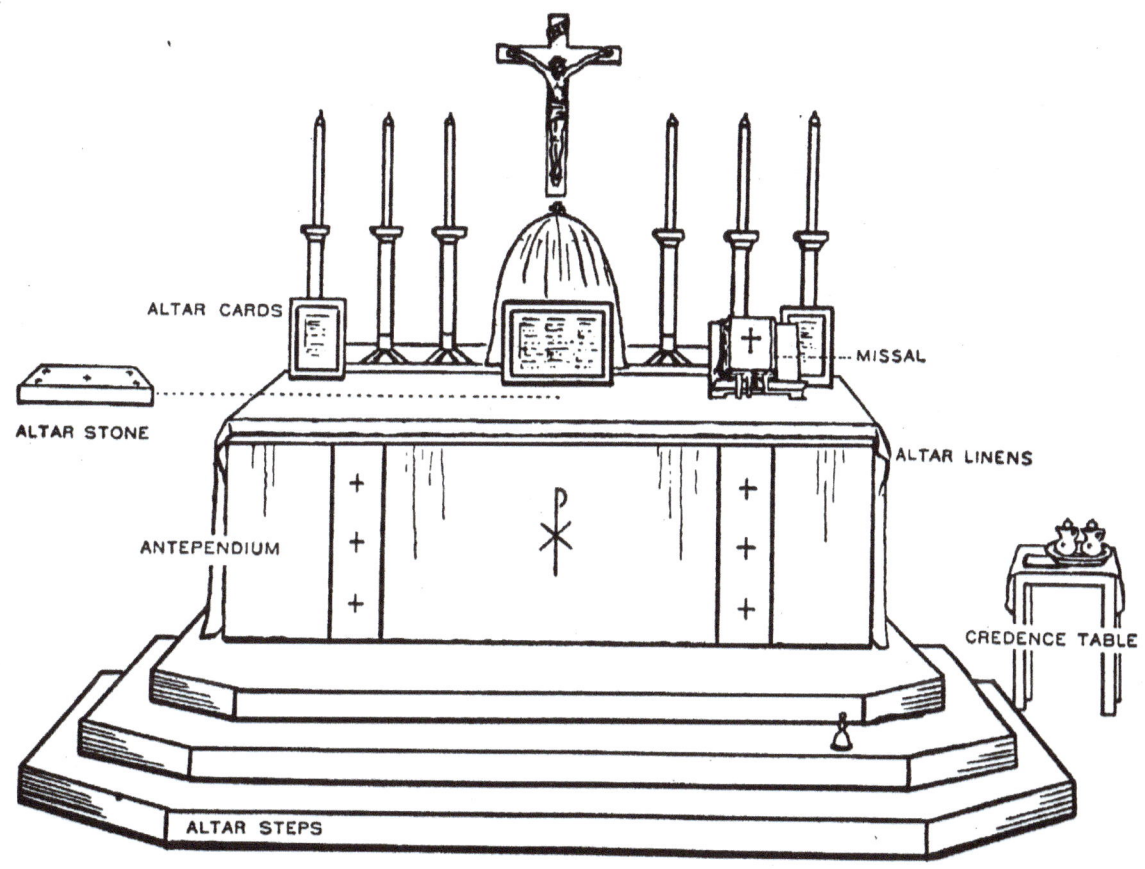

Question 17 ❖ How many candles are lit at High Mass?

Question 18 ❖ How many Altar Cloths cover the Altar?

Question 19 ❖ What is kept on the Credence Table?

Question 20 ❖ List two differences between a Sacrament and a Sacramental

Lesson 5

Level 3

Post Communion Level

Catechism

The Virtues and Gifts of the Holy Ghost

59. **What are the chief powers that are given to us with sanctifying grace?**

The chief powers that are given to us with sanctifying grace are the three theological virtues and the seven gifts of the Holy Ghost.

60. **What are the three theological virtues?**

The three theological virtues are faith, hope and charity.

61. **What is faith?**

Faith is the virtue by which we firmly believe, on the word of God, all the truths He has revealed.

It is very important to learn well and to remember the three theological virtues, that is; faith, hope and charity. The virtue of faith is very important, because without it we cannot go to heaven. Faith in God is believing in Him without actually seeing Him. We do not have faith in the existence of our mother or father because we know they exist. Having faith is believing in something or someone we cannot see.

When Saint Thomas the Apostle said he wouldn't believe that Jesus had risen unless he saw Him and touched His wounds, Our Lord rebuked him, saying, "Thomas, you believe in Me because you see Me. Blessed are they who do not see Me yet still believe". This is an important lesson for us. We must have faith in God so that one day we will live with Him forever in heaven.

Question 1 ❖ What are the three theological virtues?

Question 2 ❖ What is faith?

Question 3 ❖ What does sanctifying grace do for us?

Level 3 - Lesson 5

Prayer

Prayer for Gaining Indulgences

"My Lord and my God, I humbly beseech you that in consideration of the merits of Our Lord, Jesus Christ, You grant me all the indulgences attached to my prayers and works this day. I desire to enter into the dispositions necessary to gain these indulgences, that I may satisfy Divine justice and assist the souls in Purgatory. Amen"

Many of the prayers we have learnt in levels one and two are very common and known by most Catholics. The prayer for gaining indulgences is not as well known, but is a wonderful prayer to learn by heart and to say every morning.

An indulgence is the saying of certain prayers, or the doing of certain acts to which the Church has attached a reward; that is, time taken off Purgatory after we die. Every time we sin, even after we have been to Confession and forgiven, we have to make up for that sin either on earth (by penances) or in Purgatory (by fire).

However, if we say certain prayers, the Church has decreed that our time in Purgatory can be lessened or even avoided. This is called an Indulgence. Therefore, an indulgence is a treasure and we should try to gain all the indulgences we can.

Our prayer this lesson is a prayer that we may gain all the indulgences possible throughout the day which will lessen our time in Purgatory. So learn this prayer very well and pray it every morning. It is a good prayer to say after your Morning Offering and the Prayer to your Guardian Angel.

Question 4 ❖ When is the best time to say the Prayer for Gaining Indulgences

Question 5 ❖ We have to make up for our sins, even after they have been forgiven. Where and how are the two ways we can make up for our sins?

Question 6 ❖ What is an indulgence?

Question 7 ❖ What is another name for the Lord's Prayer?

Question 8 ❖ Write out the definition of prayer.

Bible Story

Solomon

David was succeeded by his son Solomon, who at first loved the Lord and walked in his father's footsteps. One night the Lord appeared to him, and said to him to ask whatever he wanted. Solomon asked for wisdom to rule over his people with justice. The Lord was so well pleased with this, that He gave him not only wisdom, but also riches, honor, and a long life.

One day two women came to the king asking him to decide a dispute they had. The one said: "I and this woman lived together in the same house, and we each had a baby boy. One night her child died, and while was asleep she took my boy and placed her dead child beside me in the bed. In the morning I saw that the child was not mine." The other woman denied this, and there seemed no way to settle the dispute.

Then Solomon ordered the living child to be cut in two, and half to be given to one woman and half to the other. The true mother's heart could not bear that harm should come to her darling boy, and she cried out: "My lord, give her the child, and do not kill it." But the other woman said: "Let it be divided."

Then Solomon, pointing to the true mother answered: "Give the child to this woman, for she is its mother." And the people were astonished at the wisdom of the king.

Solomon built a temple to Almighty God at Jerusalem. It was the grandest and most beautiful the world has ever seen. For twenty years Solomon did all that he could for the glory of God, but when he grew old he fell into sin and oppressed his people until they became discontented and rebellious.

Question 9 ❖ What wonderful thing did Solomon build for God?

Question 10 ❖ What gift did Solomon ask for from God?

Question 11 ❖ How did David kill Goliath?

Level 3 - Lesson 5

The Saints

Saint Aloysius Gonzaga

Aloysius was the son of a very famous and noble family. They expected him to make a name for himself in the world. Instead, he promised God he would never marry. He asked to love God and Our Lady alone. When he was very young, he became a Jesuit. From the very start, he was as holy as he could be. He kept his soul as pure as the whitest snow. He loved Mary with all his heart. He stayed for hours on his knees before Christ in the Blessed Sacrament.

But he was a very brave young man. When a terrible sickness came over the city, Aloysius went out to care for the sick. Once he brought home a very sick old man and nursed him in his own bed. He wanted very much to be a priest. But God wanted to show young people that even the very young can be saints. So he took Aloysius early with Him to Heaven. He is the special patron of boys and girls and is their model of purity.

Saint Aloysius Gonzaga Feast day is June 21st.

Question 12 ❖ Saint Aloysius is a model of what?

Question 13 ❖ What did Saint Aloysius want to become?

Question 14 ❖ What position did Saint Gregory hold in the Church?

The Fifth Station

Simon of Cyrene helps Jesus to carry His Cross

The Roman soldiers saw that with every step, Jesus was weakening. They did not want Him to die on the road; they wanted Him to die on the Cross, so they called up a man, Simon of Cyrene, to help Jesus with the Cross.

He was most unwilling, as he was only a passer-by. But when he was given the Cross, his soul was flooded with graces. It became an honor for him to help carry the Cross.

Many times Jesus asks us to carry a Cross and the best we do is to complain. Let us ask Saint Simon of Cyrene to help us to carry our crosses without complaining. Jesus gives us crosses that we might better prepare ourselves for heaven.

Question 15 ❖ Who helped Jesus to carry His Cross?

Question 16 ❖ Initially, was Simon of Cyrene willing to carry the Cross?

Question 17 ❖ Write out the first five Stations of the Cross.

Level 3 - Lesson 5

General

The Sacred Vestments

Amice: The Amice is a short, square white piece of linen, with two long tapes used to fasten it to the shoulders. Once this was worn as a hood or shawl to cover the head.

Alb: The Alb is a long, white linen garment reaching nearly to the ground. It is worn over the cassock

Cincture: The Cincture is a long white cord with two tassels. The priest wears it around his waist like a belt, to keep the alb in place.

Maniple: The Maniple is a long silk looped band that hangs from the priest's left arm. This is of the same color as that of the feast.

Stole: The stole is a long, narrow piece of silk worn around the neck. It is also of the same color as that of the feast.

Chasuble: The chasuble is the large outer garment. It is the last vestment the priest puts on. The chasuble is either white, gold, red, green, rose, violet or black depending upon the feast.

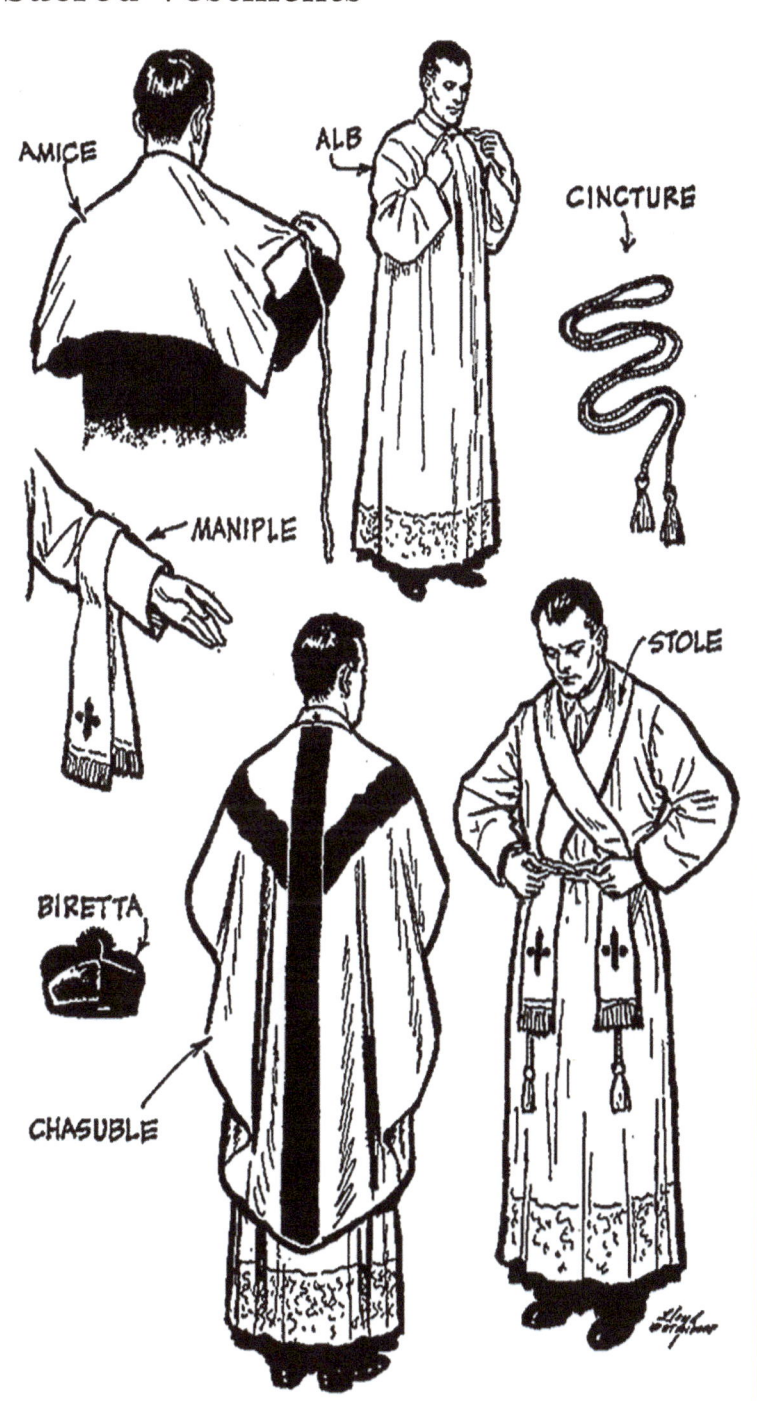

General

Vestment Colors

White: Means joy and purity. It is worn on joyful feasts of Our Lord, on feasts of the Blessed Virgin, the angels, the saints who are not martyrs and the Sundays after Easter.

Red: The color of blood and fire. It is worn on feasts of the Passion of Our Lord, the Apostles, the Martyrs, and on Pentecost

Green: The sign of hope. It is worn on Sundays after Epiphany and Pentecost

Violet: A sign of the spirit of penance. It is worn in Advent and Lent

Black: A sign of death, sorrow and mourning. It is worn on Good Friday and in Masses of the Dead

Rose: A sign of a joyous break during a period of penance. It is worn on the third Sunday of Advent, and the fourth Sunday of Lent.

Gold: Worn in the Place of White or Red for special feasts.

Question 18 ❖ What is the first vestment a priest puts on?

Question 19 ❖ What vestment is worn around the neck?

Question 20 ❖ When are red vestments worn?

Question 21 ❖ How many Altar Cloths cover the Altar?

Level 3 - Lesson 5

General

Lesson 6

Level 3

Post Communion Level

Catechism

The Virtues and the Gifts of the Holy Ghost

62. What is hope?

Hope is the virtue by which we firmly trust that God will give us eternal happiness and the means to obtain it.

63. What is Charity?

Charity is the virtue by which we love God above all things for His own sake, and our neighbor as ourselves.

64. Which are the seven gifts of the Holy Ghost?

The seven gifts of the Holy Ghost are: wisdom, understanding, counsel, fortitude, knowledge, piety and fear of the Lord.

The three theological virtues of Faith, Hope and Charity are the virtues upon which we live our entire lives. We have faith that God exists, and that He rewards the just (heaven) and punishes the wicked (hell). We hope that through living a good life God will reward us with heaven for all eternity. We love God (charity) above all things, and we try to help our neighbor to know, love and serve Him.

If we live the three theological virtues, we will live good and holy lives. One way of living these virtues is by praying daily the Acts of Faith, Hope and Charity.

The gifts of the Holy Ghost also help us to live good lives. Let us pray to the Holy Ghost often to help us use these gifts wisely.

Question 1 ❖ What is hope?

Question 2 ❖ Which are the seven gifts of the Holy Ghost?

Question 3 ❖ What are the three theological virtues?

Level 3 - Lesson 6

Prayer

Examination of Conscience

In Level One we studied the Examination of Conscience in the General Section of the course. In this lesson we are going to revise what we have already studied. The Examination of Conscience is a very important part of our prayers that should be said every night. The examination we have outlined below is a very good one you can use, but you may already be using another which is fine.

The 1st Commandment: *I am the Lord thy God; thou shalt not have strange Gods before me*

* Did I go to non-Catholic services?
* Was I willfully distracted during prayers?
* Did I bother others during prayers?
* Was I ashamed that I was a Catholic?

The 2nd Commandment: *Thou shalt not take the name of the Lord thy God in vain.*

* Did I use God's or Jesus' Holy Name in anger or fun?
* Did I curse (wish someone evil)?
* Did I make fun of holy things?

The 3rd Commandment: *Remember to keep holy the Sabbath Day*

* Did I miss Holy Mass on Sundays or holy days through my own fault?
* Did I come late to Holy Mass through my own fault?

The 4th Commandment: *Honor thy Father & thy Mother*

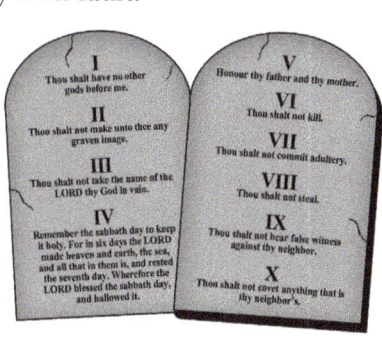

* Did I forget to pray for my parents?
* Did I disobey my parents?
* Did I disobey my teachers and priests?
* Did I make fun of old people?
* Was I mean to my parents?
* Was I mean to my teachers and priests?
* Did I wish my parents, teachers, and priests evil?

Prayer

The 5th Commandment: *Thou shalt not kill*

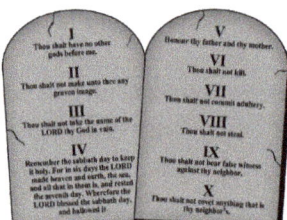

* Did I think myself better than others? (pride)
* Did I fight and quarrel with other children?
* Did I hit my brothers or sisters?
* Was I mean to other children?
* Did I call them bad names?
* Was I angry, stubborn or lazy?
* Did I eat or drink too much or hurt my body in any other way?
* Did I hate others?
* Did I try to get even with others?
* Did I lead other children into sin by my bad example?

The 6th & 9th Commandments: *Thou shalt not commit adultery. Thou shalt not covet thy neighbor's wife.*

* Did I have bad thoughts and like them?
* Did I tell rude (impure) stories?
* Did I listen to impure stories?
* Did I want to look at or do things that were not pure?
* Did I look at or draw impure pictures?

The 7th & 10th Commandments: *Thou shalt not steal. Thou shalt not covet thy neighbor's goods.*

* Did I steal anything? How much? Where from?
* Did I help others to steal? Did I tell others to steal?
* Did I take or keep stolen things given to me by others?
* Did I hurt or spoil another's property?
* Did I cheat in class or at home?
* Did I keep valuable things when found?
* Was I envious or jealous of others?

The 8th Commandment: *Thou shalt not bear false witness against thy neighbor*

* Did I tell lies?
* Did these lies hurt others?
* Did I talk about the sins of others without necessity?
* Did I say mean things about others in their absence?

Level 3 - Lesson 6

Prayer

The Commandments of the Church:

* Did I ever make a bad Confession by not being sorry for my sins?
* Did I ever make a bad Confession by keeping back a mortal sin?
* Did I ever go to Confession and not do or say my penance afterwards?
* Did I receive Holy Communion without fasting?
* Did I receive Holy Communion when I was in mortal sin?
* Did I fail to receive the Holy Sacrament of Penance once a year?
* Did I fail to receive Easter Communion at Easter time?

Question 4 ❖ When should we make our Examination of Conscience?

Question 5 ❖ What are the two major divisions that we make in making our Examination of Conscience?
Answer: We examine ourselves on the _____ Commandments and on the Commandments of the _____ .

Question 6 ❖ We have to make up for our sins, even after they have been forgiven. Where and how are the two ways we can make up for our sins?

Bible Story

The Division of the Kingdom

At Solomon's death the Jewish people divided into two kingdoms, Israel and Juda. Jerusalem remained the capital of Juda, while Samaria became the capital of Israel. The people of Israel soon fell into idolatry, and although God did much to save them, both by humbling and by cheering them, they were so self-willed and stubborn, that they would not obey His laws. At last, to punish them for their sins, He allowed the Assyrians, a pagan nation, to conquer them and make them slaves and in a short time there was nothing left of them as a nation.

The people of Juda, too, gave themselves up, for a while, to idolatry and sin. To punish them, God allowed the Babylonians to burn the Temple of Solomon, destroy Jerusalem, and, later on, to carry the entire people of Juda to Babylon where they were kept as prisoners for seventy years. At the end of that time when they were truly sorry for their sins, God led the Jews back to their own country. They at once rebuilt Jerusalem and the Temple, and for two hundred years lived peacefully and happily.

From the second century before the birth of our Saviour, the Jews suffered much at the hands of pagan nations and from rivalries among themselves. At last the Romans, then the greatest nation on the earth, were called upon to settle their disputes. Soon the Romans with their armies filled the country, seized the government, and made Herod King of the Jews. Thus ended the kingdom of Juda. The time had now come for Our Lord Jesus Christ to be born into the world to save man from sin, and open the gates of Heaven, which had been closed by the fall of our first parents.

Question 7 ❖ For how many years were the Jews taken captive to Babylon?

Question 8 ❖ Why did God allow the people of Juda to be taken captives?

Question 9 ❖ Who did the Romans make the King of the Jews?

Level 3 - Lesson 6

The Saints

Saint Catherine of Alexandria

Catherine was a very rich child, being the daughter of noble parents. She was able to go to school and studied very hard. She was always very holy. During her studies she found time to pray quietly to God.

In the days of Catherine, the Christians were being persecuted. When Catherine was 18 years old, she went to the Emperor, who was violently persecuting the Christians and told him that he must stop attacking the good people and also stop serving false gods. The Emperor was insulted and put her in gaol. He said that she must die by being tortured on a spiked wheel.

A miracle happened when she touched the wheel. It fell apart. The Emperor then ordered her head to be cut off. When her head was cut off, the angels from heaven carried her body to Mount Sinai, where later a church and convent was built in her honor.

Saint Catherine of Alexandria Feast day is November 25th.

Question 10 ❖ How old was Saint Catherine when she went to the Emperor?

Question 11 ❖ How was Saint Catherine finally martyred?

Question 12 ❖ Why is Saint Catherine depicted with a spiked wheel?

The Sixth Station

Veronica Wipes the Face of Jesus

Our Lord was comforted by this holy woman named Veronica. She saw the unjust and cruel sufferings of Jesus, and not even fearing the lash of the Roman soldiers, she broke through the line and wiped Our Lord's Sacred Face. As a reward, the image of our dear Saviour's Face was imprinted upon Veronica's cloth.

Many times in our lives, God gives us an opportunity to do something for Him. How many times do we find excuses? There are people watching! or, what will people think of me if they see me praying? or, I can't wear my scapular in public because people might laugh! and so on.

Saint Veronica is now a SAINT because she had no human respect; that is, she did not care what others thought of her, she just did it for the love of God. Oh, we have so much to learn! Let us ask Saint Veronica to help us overcome our weak human fears, and let her example, in this Station of the Cross be an example to us of what we should do to show Our Lord how much we really love Him. If we don't try to comfort and help Our Lord in His sufferings, do we really love Him?

Question 13 ❖ What reward did Jesus give to Saint Veronica for wiping His face?

Question 14 ❖ What do we mean by human respect?

Question 15 ❖ Who helped Jesus to carry His Cross?

General

Level 3 - Lesson 6

Our Sunday Best

If the Pope or the Queen came to visit your home, you would no doubt dress in your finest clothes. Mum would get out the best crockery and cutlery, you would polish your shoes, wash your face and do everything possible to look your best.

How much more should we prepare ourselves when we go to Holy Mass, particularly on a Sunday.

Thongs are great for around the home during the hot summer months, but they are not acceptable to be worn to Mass.

Only our best clothes should be worn to Sunday Mass. Yes, that means a tie for the men (and the boys), and for the girls, their best dress or skirt. Shoes should be cleaned, hair washed and our appearance should be neat and tidy.

Some children go to Mass in jeans and sports shoes. This is not showing God the respect due to Him. Let us resolve from this moment on to always prepare ourselves well for Holy Mass and to wear our Sunday Best.

Question 16 ❖ Why should we not wear thongs or such things to Mass?

Question 17 ❖ How many Altar Cloths cover the Altar?

Lesson 7

Level 3

Post Communion Level

Catechism

The Catholic Church

65. **What is the Church?**

   The Church is the congregation of all baptized persons united in the same true faith, the same sacrifice, and the same sacraments, under the Holy Father, the Pope.

66. **Why did Jesus Christ found the Church?**

   Jesus Christ founded the Church to bring all men to eternal salvation.

67. **To whom did Christ give the power to teach, to sanctify and to rule the members of His Church?**

   Christ gave the power to teach, to sanctify, and to rule the members of His Church to the apostles, the first bishops of the Church.

68. **Who are the successors of the apostles?**

   The successors of the apostles are the bishops of the Church.

When Jesus was on the Earth, He chose twelve Apostles to continue His work on Earth. He chose Saint Peter as the head of the Apostles and the first Pope.
Jesus could have decided any way to save us, but He decided that He would establish a Church. This therefore is the will of God, that we should obey Him through His Church.

Question 1 ❖ What is the Church?

Question 2 ❖ To whom did Christ give the power to teach, to sanctify and to rule the members of His Church?

Question 3 ❖ What is hope?

Level 3 - Lesson 7

Prayer

Prayer to our Patron Saint

O great Saint whose name I bear, protect me, pray for me, that like thee I may serve God faithfully on earth and glorify Him eternally with thee in heaven.
Amen.

At our baptism, we are given the name of a Saint in heaven. Some children are give a second Saint's name also. These saints become very special to us and they have a particular interest in us and in our salvation.

It is good to pray regularly to our patron saint/s that they might protect us from evil and intercede with God for us. It is also a good thing to read stories of our patrons, to know them better and to therefore imitate their virtues.

Question 4 ❖ When are we given a special patron saint to help us?

Question 5 ❖ What is the name of your patron saint?

Question 6 ❖ When should we make our Examination of Conscience?

Bible Story

Jesus Blesses the Little Children

We are going to study the New Testament for the remainder of this level. We start with the beautiful story of the love Jesus has for little children.

One day the disciples were talking to Jesus about His kingdom, and they wanted to know who would be the greatest in His kingdom. There was a little child passing at the time, and Jesus called the child to Him and said to His disciples: "Amen I say to you, unless you be converted (made good) and become as little children, you shall not enter into the kingdom of heaven."

Jesus then told them what a bad thing it was to teach sin to little children, or to another, He said that it would be better for any one teaching sin to these little ones of His, that a mill stone be tied around his neck, and that he should be drowned in the sea. You see, Jesus loved little children who were good, and grown-up people must be good too, and as simple as little children. You must never tell anything wrong to another, or teach those younger than you any sins, because you know now what Jesus said.

Jesus at this time also told fathers and mothers, husbands and wives how they should live,. There were many mothers in the crowd, and they had their little children with them. When Jesus had done speaking, the mothers brought their little children to Jesus, that He might lay His hands upon them and bless them; but the disciples thought it was too much trouble for Jesus, so they told the mothers not to bring the children. But Jesus was not pleased at this, for He loved little children, and He said: "Suffer the little children, and forbid them not to come to Me, for the kingdom of heaven is for such." And then Jesus blessed each little child. Little children ought to love Jesus very much for this.

Question 7	❖	What did Jesus say after He said, "Unless you be converted and become as little children…"
Question 8	❖	What did Jesus say when the Apostles tried to forbid the children from coming to Him?
Question 9	❖	Who did the Romans make the King of the Jews?

The Saints

Saint Francis Xavier

Saint Francis Xavier went to the University of Paris. He was a champion runner. He was a great athlete. But he was a very clever student, too. In class, he was the leader. He learned easily. He studied hard. "I want to be a great professor," he said. "I want to know all there is to know. I want people to listen when I talk. I want to write wonderful books."

Then he met Saint Ignatius Loyola. "What good will it do you, " Ignatius asked him, "if you win the whole world and then lose your soul?" Francis thought this over. He decided he could win the world and at the same time save his soul. So he became a friend of Saint Ignatius. He became a Jesuit. "Send me out," he said, "and I will win the world for our dear Lord."
So Saint Ignatius Loyola sent him out as a missionary. He went to India. He told people there about Jesus. He went to Japan. The pagans listened. Many of them too became Catholics. Then he wanted to go to China. However, he died on a little island just off the coast of China.

But he had converted thousands and thousands. He was the greatest missionary since the days of the Apostles.

Saint Francis Xavier Feast day is 3rd of December
and
he is one of the principal patrons of Australia.

Question 10 ❖ Name two countries where Saint Francis Xavier went.

Question 11 ❖ Of what country is Saint Francis Xavier a patron?

Question 12 ❖ Of what Order did Saint Francis Xavier belong?

Question 13 ❖ Why is Saint Catherine depicted with a spiked wheel?

The Seventh Station

Jesus Falls the Second Time

At each step, Our Blessed Saviour was growing weaker. The scourging, the crown of thorns, the rough and heavy cross, the sins of the world all weighed down upon Him and He fell a second time.

The Roman soldiers were very worried that He wouldn't make it to the place of execution, but Our Lord picked Himself up and continued on this Sacred road to His crucifixion. Let us never give up, no matter how difficult. Our Lord has given us the example to follow.

If we ever fall into sin, we need to go to Confession and rise anew in our good resolutions.

Question 14 ❖ What is the seventh Station of the Cross?

Question 15 ❖ What should we do if we fall into sin?

Question 16 ❖ What reward did Jesus give to Saint Veronica for wiping His face?

Level 3 - Lesson 7

General

The Spiritual Works of Mercy

In Level Two we studied in detail the seven Corporal Works of Mercy. In this Level we are going to examine the seven Spiritual Works of Mercy. They are listed below and should be learnt by heart.

The Corporal and Spiritual works of Mercy work together. Man is made of a body and soul; we must therefore help others spiritually as well as bodily.

The chief spiritual works of mercy are:

1. To admonish the sinner

2. To instruct the ignorant

3. To counsel the doubtful

4. To comfort the sorrowful

5. To bear wrongs patiently

6. To forgive all injuries

7. To pray for the living and the dead

Question 17 ❖ How many spiritual works of mercy are there?

Question 18 ❖ Man is made up of what?

Question 19 ❖ Why should we not wear thongs or such things to Mass?

Question 20 ❖ What vestment is worn around the neck?

Lesson 8

Level 3

Post Communion Level

Catechism

The Catholic Church

69. **Did Christ give special power in His Church to any one of the Apostles?**

    Christ gave special power in His Church to Saint Peter by making him the head of the apostles and the chief teacher and ruler of the entire Church.

70. **Who is the successor of Saint Peter?**

    The successor of Saint Peter is the Holy Father, the Bishop of Rome.

71. **Who helps the bishops in the care of souls?**

    The priests, especially parish priests, help the bishops in the care of souls.

Last lesson we learnt that Our Lord started up the Church in order to gain souls for heaven. Let us learn this lesson, more about this Church. We must always remember that it was Christ Himself who decided to start the Catholic Church, so we must listen to her and obey her as if it were Christ Himself speaking to us.

The catechism questions this week show us the structure of the Church as chosen by Christ. That is, the Pope (Bishop of Rome) is the visible head of the Church and his helpers are the priests and bishops. Let us always keep the clergy (the pope, bishops and priests) in our prayers.

Question 1 ❖ Who is the successor of Saint Peter?

Question 2 ❖ Who helps the bishops in the care of souls?

Question 3 ❖ To whom did Christ give the power to teach, to sanctify and to rule the members of His Church?

Level 3 - Lesson 8

Prayer

Who loves our dear Lord more than His holy Mother, Mary? Like at the Marriage Feast of Cana, whatever Mary asks of Jesus, He cannot refuse her. Jesus loves His Blessed Mother so much that He always gives her what she asks, and in turn, our Blessed Mother only asks for things that are important and good for our souls.

It follows then, that we should pray to Our Lady and ask her for all the things we need, temporal and spiritual. If these things are good for us and of benefit for our souls, Mary will ask Jesus for the things we need. And of course, Jesus never refuses His Mother.

Saint Bernard had a very strong devotion to the Mother of God. He always prayed to her and asked her for the many things he needed. In fact, he wrote the beautiful prayer, The Memorare. It is a prayer of petition, and one for us to learn and to use often. Our Lady desires that we pray to her. She wants to help us, and is only waiting for us to ask for her help.

MEMORARE

Remember, O most gracious Virgin Mary, that never was it known that anyone who fled to thy protection, implored thy help, or sought thine intercession was left unaided. Inspired by this confidence, I fly unto thee, O Virgin of virgins, my mother; to thee do I come, before thee I stand, sinful and sorrowful. O Mother of the Word Incarnate, despise not my petitions, but in thy mercy hear and answer me. Amen.

Question 4 ❖ Who made up the prayer, the Memorare?

Question 5 ❖ What type of prayer is the Memorare?

Question 6 ❖ What are the two major divisions that we make in making our Examination of Conscience?

We examine ourselves on the _____ Commandments and on the Commandments of the _____ .

Bible Story

Jesus Walks on Water

One day, Jesus told His disciples to go in a boat across the lake and wait for Him. Jesus liked to pray alone, so he sent away all the people and the disciples. The disciples waited for Jesus in the boat, and a storm came on with the night. Now, Jesus saw the boat on the lake, and He knew they were afraid, so He walked out on the sea – He did not swim, but walked on the water, just as we walk on land.

When the disciples saw Jesus coming to them in this strange way, they were afraid, and they said to one another: "It is a ghost." But Jesus spoke to them, saying: "Be of good heart: it is I, fear not." And Peter, who was in the boat, said: "Lord, if it be Thou, bid me come to Thee upon the waters;" and Jesus said: "Come." Peter, who saw how rough the sea was, and how the wind blew, was afraid, but he stepped out of the boat, and when he began to sink, he cried out, saying: "Lord, save me."

And at once Jesus put out His hand and took hold of Peter's saying: "Oh, thou of little faith, why didst thou doubt?" They walked together to the boat, and the wind ceased. The disciples, when they saw this, adored Jesus, and said: "Indeed, Thou art the Son of God."

Question 7 ❖ Why did Saint Peter sink?

Question 8 ❖ Why did Jesus say, "Oh thou of little faith"?

Question 9 ❖ What did Jesus say when the Apostles tried to forbid the children from coming to Him?

The Saints

Saint Nicholas de Flue

Saint Nicholas de Flue is perhaps the most important figure in the history of Switzerland. He was a soldier and a great patriot. It is probably due to him that the Swiss Confederation was preserved, such was his gift of pacifying opposing factions.

Saint Nicholas took a wife and she bore him ten children, yet, one of the most amazing things happened when he attained the age of fifty. He felt that he had the vocation of a hermit and retired into complete solitude with the perfect consent of the family. Things like this can only happen when grace is so abundant that it minimizes any doubt as to the heavenly inspiration of such a tremendous decision.

It is reported that for many years Saint Nicholas was unable to ingest any food whatsoever and he lived solely on nourishment he received from the Holy Eucharist. A chapel had been built next to his hermitage and a priest celebrates Mass in that chapel every day.

Saint Nicholas was canonized in 1947, by Pope Pius XII and is the patron saint of Switzerland

Saint Nicholas De Flue Feast day is 25th September

Question 10 ❖ Which country is Saint Nicholas of Flue the patron?

Question 11 ❖ What amazing thing happened to Saint Nicholas when he was fifty years of age?

Question 12 ❖ What miracle took place for many years in the life of Saint Nicholas de Flue?

Question 13 ❖ Name two countries where Saint Francis Xavier went.

The Eighth Station

The Women of Jerusalem Weep over Jesus

A number of women from Jerusalem were following Jesus during His Sacred Passion, weeping over the cruel sufferings he was undergoing. Jesus turned to them and said, "daughters of Jerusalem, weep not for Me, but for yourselves and for your children."

Our Lord was prophesising the destruction of Jerusalem which would take place some forty years later (70AD).

Our Lord is telling us in this Station of the Cross to be more concerned with our souls than with anything else.

Like the women of Jerusalem, let us follow Our Lord in His Sacred Passion.

Question 14 ❖ Write out the first eight Stations of the Cross

Question 15 ❖ What did Jesus say to the women of Jerusalem?

Level 3 - Lesson 8

The 1st Spiritual Work of Mercy

To Admonish the Sinner

To admonish the sinner means to reprimand the person who is sinning, and to show them the errors in what they are doing. Those in authority, such as parents and teachers, are bound to admonish those under them of their sins and even their faults.

For children, one way to admonish the sinner is by giving good example. If someone came into the school grounds one day and started showing bad magazines, you could just leave and say to your friends, "Let's go from here, for this is not pleasing to God".

A parent or teacher, when admonishing the sinner, must do so with gentleness and charity. This is the most effective way of bringing a soul back to God. Saint James says, (James: 5:20) "He who causes a sinner to be brought back from his misguided way, will save his soul."

Saint Ambrose admonishing the Emperor Theodosius for the unjust killing of 7,000 people.

Question 16 ❖ How can a child admonish a sinner?

Question 17 ❖ What do we mean by the word admonish?

Question 18 ❖ When are black vestments worn?

Lesson 9

Level 3

Post Communion Level

Catechism

The Marks of the Church

72. Which is the one true Church established by Christ?

The one true Church established by Christ is the Catholic Church.

73. How do we know that the Catholic Church is the one true Church established by Christ?

We know that the Catholic Church is the one true Church established by Christ because it alone has the marks of the true Church.

74. What are the chief marks of the Church?

The chief marks of the Church are four: It is One, Holy, Catholic and Apostolic.

75. Are all obliged to belong to the Catholic Church in order to be saved?

All are obliged to belong to the Catholic Church, in some way, in order to be saved. Our Lord Jesus Christ came onto this earth to open for us the gates of heaven, and to show us how to live our lives and save our souls. He did this by establishing the Church. The devil so loves to confuse us that he has caused many breakaway churches to be founded. Many people today are uncertain as to which is the true Church of Jesus Christ, which is, of course, the Catholic Church. Study well the above catechism questions as they show how we can see that the Catholic Church is the true Church founded by our Saviour.

Question 1	❖	How do we know that the Catholic Church is the one true Church established by Christ?
Question 2	❖	What are the chief marks of the Church?
Question 3	❖	Who is the successor of Saint Peter?

Level 3 - Lesson 9

Prayer

The Act of Faith
O my God, I firmly believe all the truths that the holy Catholic Church believes and teaches. I believe these truths O Lord, because You, the infallible Truth has revealed them to her.
In this faith I am resolved to live and die. *Amen.*

The Act of Hope
O my God, relying on Your promises, I hope that through the Infinite merits of Jesus Christ, You might grant me pardon of my sins and the graces necessary to serve You in this life and to obtain eternal happiness in the next. *Amen.*

The Act of Charity
O my God, I love You with all my heart because You are infinitely good and perfect, and I love my neighbor as myself for love of You. Grant that I may love You more and more in this life and in the next for all eternity. *Amen.*

In Level One, we learnt the Acts of Faith, Hope and Charity. In this lesson we are going to revise these prayers. They are very important prayers, because when we pray them we are showing our belief in the three theological virtues; that of faith, hope and charity. These prayer are best said during our Morning or Night Prayers, but can be said at any time, especially when we have need for one of these virtues. These three virtues are the most fundamental of all the virtues, but Saint Paul tells us that the greatest of these virtues is Charity. Let us therefore practice charity all our lives. (Charity is the love of God and the love of our neighbor for the love of God).

Question 4   ❖   What are the three theological virtues?

Question 5   ❖   What is the greatest of these virtues?

Question 6   ❖   Write out the Act of Charity

Question 7   ❖   Who made up the prayer, the Memorare?

Bible Story

The Blind Man

When Jesus and His apostles had come to a town called Jericho with a number of people, a blind man who heard that Jesus was passing, called out to Him saying: "Jesus, Son of David, have mercy on me." And Jesus stood still, and told them to bring the blind man to Him; so the people brought the blind man, and Jesus said to him: "What is it that you want me to do for you?" and the blind man said: "Master, that I may see." Then Jesus said to him: "Go on your way, you faith has made you whole." and at once the blind man could, and he followed Jesus with the other people.

Question 8 ❖ Who cured the blind man in Jericho?

Question 9 ❖ What did Jesus say when He cured the man?

Question 10 ❖ Why did Jesus say to Saint Peter, "Oh thou of little faith"?

Level 3 - Lesson 9

The Saints

Saint Jane Frances De Chantal

Here is a wonderful saint. She was a saint as a little girl. She was a saint as a wife. When she was a widow, she was a saint. Then she became a nun and was a saint in the convent. When she was a very little girl, Jane Frances asked Our Lady to take care of her. Our Lady always did. Then she married a nobleman. She made him a beautiful home. She loved her husband. She was devoted to her children. But sorrow came to her. Her good husband died. Two children and a sister died. Her friends told her to marry again. She was sad and her life was very hard. At last her children grew up. She knew that God wanted her to be a nun. So with St. Francis De Sales she started the Visitation Order. Her daughters, the Visitation Sisters, to this day pray, do penance, and teach children to love and serve God as

Jane Frances did.

Saint Jane Frances De Chantal Feast day is August 21st.

Question 11 ❖ What did Saint Jane Frances De Chantal do after her husband died?

Question 12 St ❖ What was the name of the Order started by St Francis De Sales and Jane Frances De Chantal?

Question 13 ❖ Of what country is Saint Nicholas De Flue the patron?

The Ninth Station

Jesus Falls the Third Time

Jesus was now nearing the hill of Calvary. At every step He was weakening. For the third time He fell to the ground with the great weight of the Cross falling upon Him. As He looked up He could see the place of execution. Despite His suffering, He arose again to continue His journey.

Let us learn from this Station to do everything for God; to continue on our journey to heaven, despite all the difficulties (falls) we endure. We should ever have before our eyes, our goal – heaven. Let us ask Jesus to give us strength to always do His Will.

Question 14 ❖ How many times did Jesus fall on His way to Calvary?

Question 15 ❖ What is the fourth Station of the Cross?

Question 16 ❖ What reward did Jesus give to Saint Veronica for wiping His face?

The 2nd Spiritual Work of Mercy

To Instruct the Ignorant

Missionaries, catechists, confessors, teachers and Catholic writers – all who teach religion or other useful knowledge – are doing an important work of mercy, and will receive a reward. They that instruct many in justice will shine as stars for all eternity. (Dan 12:3). Those who collect money for foreign missions also do this work of mercy.

It is a great grace to instruct a soul in the knowledge and love of God. The Catholic teacher practices this spiritual work of mercy every day. Of course, a priest, brother or nun live this spiritual work every day of their lives.

Question 17 ❖ To teach religion is what Spiritual Work of Mercy?

Question 18 ❖ What occupation practices the Second Spiritual Work of Mercy every day?

Question 19 ❖ What do we mean by the word admonish?

Lesson 10

Level 3
Post Communion Level

Catechism

The Communion of Saints and the Forgiveness of Sins

76. What is meant by "the communion of saints" in the Apostles' Creed?

By "the communion of saints" is meant the union of the faithful on earth, the blessed in heaven, and the souls in purgatory, with Christ as their Head.

77. What is meant in the Apostles' Creed by "the forgiveness of sins"?

By "the forgiveness of sins" in the Apostles' Creed is meant that God has given to the Church, through Jesus Christ, the power to forgive sins.

This lesson we only have two questions to learn; but they are both very important. The Communion of Saints is the Church on Earth, the Church in Purgatory and the Church in Heaven. Together, they make up the Church of God.

The Church on Earth is called the Church Militant (this means the Church fighting – for our souls). The Church in Purgatory is called the Church Suffering (they are assured of their salvation, but are suffering in the fires of Purgatory). The Church in Heaven is called the Church Triumphant (they have received their reward).

Each section of the Church can help others; that is, the Saints in heaven can help those in Purgatory or on Earth, the Souls in Purgatory can help those on the Earth, and those on the Earth can help the Souls in Purgatory. But the Souls in Purgatory cannot help themselves.

The second question explains that Our Lord has given the Catholic Church the power to forgive sins – the Sacrament of Penance.

Question 1 ❖ What is meant by "the communion of saints" in the Apostles' Creed?

Question 2 ❖ What do we call the Church on Earth?

Question 4 ❖ What do we call the Church in Heaven?

Question 5 ❖ Are all obliged to belong to the Catholic Church in order to be saved?

Level 3 - Lesson 10

Prayer

Prayer for the Pope

Let us pray for our most Holy Father the Pope (say the name of the Pope here), may the Lord preserve him and give him life and make him blessed upon the earth and deliver him not up to the will of his enemies. Amen.

From the time of the first Pope, Saint Peter, Our Lord has ensured that His Church has always been with a visible leader, the Pope. Of course Our Lord Himself is the Head of the Church, but He has given us a leader here on Earth. We need to pray for the Pope every day, that the Lord gives him all the graces he needs for this most difficult job he has. We would be very poor Catholics indeed if we did not remember to pray for God's vicar on earth – the Pope.

In this prayer, we pray that not only will God give him all the graces he needs, but that God will protect him against his enemies. If you have not been in the habit of praying for the Pope, it is a habit you should start to foster. God will grant us good and holy Popes if enough people pray hard.

Question 6 ❖ Who was the first Pope?

Question 8 ❖ List four things we are asking for when we pray for the Pope.

Question 9 ❖ Write out the Prayer for the Pope.

Question 10 ❖ What are the three theological virtues?

Bible Story

The Good Samaritan

At times the people and apostles could not understand Jesus, and He would then explain what He meant by telling them stories. We call these parables.

Once when Jesus was teaching, a man who was a lawyer thought he would tempt Jesus, so he said to Him: "Master, what must I do to possess eternal life?" And Jesus said: "What is written in the law? How readest thou?" And the lawyer said: "It is written: Thou shalt love the Lord thy God with thy whole heart, and with thy whole soul, and with all thy strength, and with all thy mind: and thy neighbor as thyself." And Jesus said: "Thou hast answered right; this do, and thou shalt live." And the man said. "Who is my neighbor?" Jesus then told him this story: Once there was a man who was going a journey from Jerusalem to Jericho, and on his way some robbers met him. They tore off all his clothes, took his money, and struck him and hurt him, so that they left him like a dead man by the side of the road. After a time, a priest went down the same way and, seeing him, passed by. In like manner, a Levite, when he was near the place and saw him and passed by. But at last a Samaritan, being on his journey, came near him, and seeing him was moved with pity, and going up to him, bound up his wounds, pouring in oil and wine, and putting the man on his own mule, brought him to an inn, and took care of him.

The next day he had to go away, but he left money with the owner of the inn, and told him to take care of the man, and that if it was not enough money, he would give him more on his return.

Then Jesus said to the lawyer: "Which of these three, in your opinion, was neighbor to him that fell among the robbers?" and he answered: "He that showed mercy to him." Then Jesus said to him: "Go, and do in like manner."

In this story Jesus teaches us who is our neighbor, and that we should do to others what we would like them to do to us. If you were hurt or sick you would like someone to be kind to you; you ought then to be always kind to others; to the ugly, dirty, and cross, as well as to those you dislike, because they are your neighbors. A neighbor in this sense does not mean only the person who lives next door, but every man, woman and child.

Question 11 ❖ What do we call stories that Jesus told?

Question 12 ❖ What was the lawyer's answer to the question, "What must I do to possess eternal life"?

Question 13 ❖ What did the Samaritan do that the priest and Levite didn't do?

Question 14 ❖ What did Jesus say when he cured the blind man?

The Saints

Saint Bridget of Sweden

Bridget was born to wealth and aristocracy which never went to her head. She was a model for Christian wives and mothers and gave birth to eight children. When she was widowed at forty, she became totally dedicated to the poor and oppressed and founded a holy Order of dedicated women. Bridget was therefore not only a selfless great helper of the poor, but she also rose to the most exalted heights of mystical wisdom and love.

The Collect prayer for her feast reads:

"O Lord God, who through Thine only begotten Son, didst reveal secrets of heaven to blessed Bridget; grant, through her loving intercession, that we Thy servants may rejoice with gladness at the revelation of Thine eternal glory. Through the same Lord. Amen."

Saint Bridget feast day is 8th of October

Question 15 ❖ What did Saint Bridget do after she was widowed?

Question 16 ❖ What was the name of the Order started by St Francis De Sales and St Jane Frances De Chantal?

The Tenth Station

Jesus is Stripped of His Garments

Jesus had arrived at the base of Calvary. He was exhausted and was suffering very much from the scourging and the crown of thorns. After the Roman soldiers took the Cross from Him, they stripped Him of His garments.

This stripping of Our Lord's clothes caused Him immense suffering. It reopened all the wounds of His scourging; but never a word of complaint escaped the lips of our Divine Saviour.

He stood near the Cross, offering Himself to the Eternal Father for our salvation.

Let us ask Jesus in this Station, that we offer ourselves to Him whenever we face pain or suffering of any type. And let us tell Jesus that we will always love Him.

Question 17 ❖ Write out the first ten Stations of the Cross

Question 18 ❖ Why did the stripping of Our Lord's garments cause Him so much suffering?

Level 3 - Lesson 10

The 3rd Spiritual Work of Mercy

To Counsel the Doubtful

The devil loves to see people have doubts about their faith. To doubt the faith is one of the most difficult trials a Catholic can face. What a great thing it is when we can counsel those who have doubts. Of course, before we can do this, we need to learn our holy faith ourselves. As in admonishing sinners, advising the doubtful should be done prudently and gently, to effect good results. It is seldom effective to rush into heated argument. Let us pray first before giving counsel.

Question 19 ❖ What should we do before we give counsel to others?

Question 20 ❖ What is one of the most difficult things a Catholic can face?

Question 21 ❖ To teach religion is what Spiritual Work of Mercy?

Lesson 11

Level 3

Post Communion Level

Catechism

The Resurrection and Life Everlasting

78. What is meant by "the resurrection of the body"?

By "the resurrection of the body" is meant that at the end of the world the bodies of all men will rise from the earth and be united again to their souls, nevermore to be separated.

79. Has the body of any human person ever been taken into heaven?

By the special favor of her Assumption, the body of the Blessed Virgin Mary was raised from the dead and taken into heaven.

80. What is the judgment called which will be passed on all men immediately after the general resurrection?

The judgment which will be passed on all men immediately after the general resurrection is called the general judgment.

The four last things ever to be remembered are death, judgment, heaven and hell. No man can escape any of these things. It doesn't matter how great we may have been in life, or how insignificant, death, judgment heaven or hell will come to us all. We must live our life, so our death will be holy, so that upon being judged, we will fly to heaven and avoid hell. The simplest layman and the greatest Pope must ever remember these four last things.

Immediately after we die we will be judged by God; this is called the particular judgment. If we are in the state of grace, our souls will go to purgatory or directly to heaven (if we have paid for all our sins), while our bodies will be buried in the earth. It is not until the general judgment that our bodies will be reunited with our souls for all eternity.

Question 1 ❖ What is the judgment called which will be passed on all men immediately after the general resurrection?

Question 2 ❖ Has the body of any human person ever been taken into heaven?

Question 3 ❖ What is meant by "the communion of saints" in the Apostles' Creed?

Level 3 - Lesson 11

Prayer

Prayer for the Conversion of Australia

O God Who hast appointed Mary Help of Christians, Saint Francis Xavier and Saint Therese of the Infant Jesus, patrons of Australia, grant, that through their intercession, our brethren outside the Church may receive the light of faith so that Australia may become one in Faith under one shepherd, through Christ our Lord. Amen

God not only expects that we love and honor our parents, but that we love and honor our country. This is true patriotism. We do not love any bad laws passed, but we pray that those making the laws will be inspired by God to do the right thing, and that they will listen to God's inspirations. This prayer is often prayed at Benediction, but it can be prayed at any time. Often after the prayer, we make the following invocations:

Mary, Help of Christians, pray for us

Saint Francis Xavier, pray for us

Saint Therese of the Infant Jesus, pray for us

Question 4 ❖ When is the Prayer for the Conversion of Australia often prayed?

Question 5 ❖ What invocations often follow the Prayer for the Conversion of Australia?

Question 6 ❖ Write out the Prayer for the Pope.

Bible Story

The Lost Sheep

Once, when Jesus was teaching, a number of men who were sinners came to Him to hear Him, and there were present also some men who thought themselves very good. These men complained because Jesus spoke to and ate with sinners; so Jesus told these men some stories.

Once there was a man who owned a hundred sheep, and he was called a shepherd. He had a hundred sheep in a fold, and one day one little lamb got out of the fold and was lost. The shepherd left all the other sheep and went to look for this lamb. At last he found it, and the poor little sheep was tired, so he took it on his shoulders and carried it back to the fold.

Then the shepherd, going home, told his friends he had found the lost sheep, and he said to them: "Rejoice with me, because I have found my sheep that was lost."

Jesus told them what this story meant: that Heaven was like the sheepfold and that the sheep were the good people, and that the lost sheep was a wicked person, one who had once been good, but had become bad. The Shepherd was God, Who went searching for the lost soul (sheep) And Jesus further said that there was more joy in Heaven at one sinner becoming good and doing penance, than over ninety-nine good people who need not penance

Question 7 ❖ How many sheep did the shepherd have?

Question 8 ❖ How many sheep got lost?

Question 9 ❖ What does this parable (story) mean?

The Saints

Saint Margaret Mary

We all know how much God loves us. He created us out of nothing. He died for our sakes. He stays with us in the Blessed Sacrament.

But men and women forget God so quickly. He asks them to love Him. Instead, they love all kinds of sinful and silly things.

Once, there was a very holy nun named Sister Margaret Mary. She loved our dear Lord with all her heart. She was sorry that everyone did not love Him too.

One day He appeared to her. He showed her His Sacred Heart. "Behold the heart that has loved men so much." He said. And He asked her to tell others about His love for them. So Saint Margaret Mary told everyone about the Sacred Heart. She loved Jesus with all her heart herself. She brought millions to love Him too.

Saint Margaret Mary is the Saint of the Heart of Jesus

Saint Margaret Mary Feast day is October 17th

Question 10 ❖ Who appeared to Saint Margaret Mary?

Question 11 ❖ Whose feast day is on October 17th?

Question 12 ❖ What did Saint Bridget do after she was widowed?

The Eleventh Station

Jesus is Nailed to the Cross

After the soldiers stripped the garments from Jesus, they laid Him on the Cross and cruelly nailed Him to it. The soldiers were amazed because Jesus did not utter one word of complaint. Every other person who had been crucified had sworn, blasphemed and fought against the soldiers. But Jesus gave up His own life; the Roman soldiers did not take it from Him.
Jesus stretched out His arms and offered up His sufferings to His Father in heaven.
When we are suffering and sometimes complain, let us think of dear Jesus being nailed to the Cross and let us promise Him we will try harder.

Question 13 ❖ Did the soldiers take Jesus' life or did Jesus give up His own life?

Question 14 ❖ Who nailed Jesus to the Cross?

Question 15 ❖ Why did the stripping of Our Lord's garments cause Him so much suffering?

Level 3 - Lesson 11

The 4th Spiritual Work of Mercy

To Comfort the Sorrowful

We can comfort those in sorrow by showing them sincere sympathy, by suggesting consolations, and by helping them in their need.

To give comfort, we may speak of God's providence and His goodness, of His love for every single one of His creatures, and of the happiness He reserves for us in heaven, when all earthly sorrows and troubles will be ended.

Question 16 ❖ What is the fourth Spiritual Work of Mercy?

Question 17 ❖ When will all earthly sorrows and troubles be ended?

Lesson 12

Level 3

Post Communion Level

Catechism

The Resurrection and Life Everlasting

81. **What is the judgment called which will be passed on each one of us immediately after death?**

    The judgment which will be passed on each one of us immediately after death is called the particular judgment.

82. **What are the rewards or punishments appointed for men after the particular judgment?**

    The rewards or punishments appointed for men after the particular judgment are heaven, purgatory, or hell.

83. **What is meant by the word "Amen" with which we end the Apostles' Creed?**

    By the word "Amen," with which we end the Apostles' Creed, is meant "So it is," or "So be it."

We learnt in an earlier level that God made us to know, love and serve Him in this world and to be happy with Him forever in the next. How we live our lives is how we will die. If we try hard to love and serve God all our lives, He will give us the grace to die a holy death. Nothing else matters in this life for us except that our souls be in the state of grace at the moment of our death.

There have been great and mighty kings who are recorded in the pages of history books, musicians, poets, architects, inventors and so on. We have all read about these great people, but where are they now? Did they die in the state of grace? This will all be revealed at the general judgment. It doesn't matter how well known or how hidden a person's life has been. All that matters is have they saved their soul?

Question 1 ❖ What is the judgment called which will be passed on each one of us immediately after death?

Question 2 ❖ What is the most important thing for every person to do in this life?

Question 3 ❖ What is meant by "the resurrection of the body"?

Level 3 - Lesson 12

Prayer

Aspirations

This lesson we are revisiting something already covered in Level One; a prayer called an Aspiration or sometimes called an ejaculatory prayer. We sometimes only think of prayer as the well known prayers such as the Our Father, Hail Mary, etc. These prayers are excellent of course, but there are many other types of prayer, e.g. meditation, aspirations, contemplation. Meditation and contemplation we will deal with in future levels, but we will concentrate this lesson on Aspirations. We read in the lives of many saints that their whole day was a prayer and we sometimes wonder how it is possible! To pray all day while at school or work! Well, one of the ways the saints prayed all day was by the use of aspirations. Some saints said as many as a thousand aspirations a day. Well, what are aspirations? They are simple, short prayers often of petition, (but can be of thanks, praise or reparation), invoking Our Lord, Our Lady or one of the saints. Examples are:

 My Jesus, mercy;
 Mary help me;
Saint Anthony, please help me find …..
 Thank You Lord;
and so on. There are no set words, they are usually said silently and come from the heart. Make aspirations part of your day. They are a constant reminder of the presence of God.

Start your day with simple yet powerful prayers:
Forgive me Lord,
Guide me Lord,
Protect me Lord,
Bless me Lord,
Thankyou Lord,
Amen

Question 4   ❖   What is another word for an Aspiration?

Question 5   ❖   Write three Aspirations you say or will try to start saying.

Question 6   ❖   What is an Aspiration?

Question 7   ❖   What invocations often follow the Prayer for the Conversion of Australia?

Bible Story

The Prodigal Son

Another story was: That once a man had two sons. He was a rich man, had a grand house, and lived in great estate. But the youngest son thought the house and life too quiet: he wanted to go out into the world and enjoy himself, and have a good time. One day he came to his father, and said: "I know you are going to divide some money between my elder brother and me; give me my share now, and let me go away." The father was pained at this, still he did not refuse his son, but gave him his share of money. After a few days this young son said good-bye to his father and brother, and took with him all his belongings, and left his father's house. He went away to a country a long way off, and there led a very bad, wicked life. In a short time he had spent all his money, and, you may be quite sure, his friends then left him, because he could treat them no more. What could he do then? He was in a strange country, and he had no money. At last he was truly miserable-he was hungry, and had no clothes. One day he went to a man and asked him for work; but he looked so poor and dirty that the man said: "I can give you no work in my house, but you may go to my farm and mind the pigs." So he went and minded the pigs, but he got no food except what the pigs did not like.

This he found so hard, and he was so miserable, that he began to think of home, and of the servants that his father had; and he said to himself: "How many servants in my father's house eat bread, and I am here dying of hunger!" So he said: "I will arise and will go to my father, and say to him: Father, I have sinned against heaven and before God, I am not worthy to be called you son; make me as one of your hired servants." He started at once on his journey to his father.

The father loved his son, and used to look out every evening for him, hoping he would come back. One evening he was looking out as usual, and he saw, a great way off, his son, and he went to meet him, and running up to him, put his arms round his neck and kissed him. But the son fell on his knees and said to him: "Father, I have sinned against heaven and before God, I am not worthy to be called your son." But the father was so glad to see him that he kissed him again and again, and put fine clothes on him, and told his servants to make a great feast, because his son who was lost, and was as dead, was found again. Then they had a great feast, and music and dancing. The elder son, who was out at work in a field, heard the music, and came to the house to see what it all meant. And the servant told him: "Your brother has returned and your father has made a great feast because he has come back safe." At this the elder brother was very angry, and he would not go into the house. His father hearing it came out to him, and tried to coax him in; but he would not, and said to his father: "I have done all you asked me to do for so many years, and have been good, and have not spent your money, but you never made a feast for me as you have for my brother, who spent all his money, and led a bad life." But the father said to him: "Son, you are always with me, and all I have is yours; but it was fit that we should make merry and be glad, for this your brother was dead and is come to life again, he was lost and is found.

Level 3 - Lesson 12

Bible Story

This story, too, was told to teach us that God will forgive sinners; but we must be sorry as the young son was, and confess our sins to the priest, as he did to his father; and as he was willing to be a servant in his father's house because of his sins, so we must be humble, and willing to suffer for our sins.

The good son, you see, was doubly rewarded, for the father said, "Son, all I have is yours"—not only his own share.

Question 8 ❖ Who does the father in this story represent?

Question 9 ❖ Who does the Prodigal Son in this story represent?

Question 10 ❖ What did the father say to the good son after he complained?

Question 11 ❖ How many sheep did the good shepherd have?

The Saints

Saint Martin of Tours

The father and mother of Martin did not believe in God. So when Martin wanted to become a Christian, they wouldn't let him. Instead, his father put him into the army when he was only fifteen. Martin was a good soldier. Though most of the soldiers were not Christians, he loved Our Lord.

One winter night, Martin met a poor beggar, freezing in the snow. Martin had no money so he took his sword, cut his cloak in half and gave one half to the beggar. That night, Our Lord came to him wearing the half cloak. He heard Jesus say to the angels, "Look, though Martin is not yet baptized, he gave Me his garment." So Martin became a Christian and converted his parents too. Because he was brave and strong, the people asked him to stop being a soldier and become their bishop. He did. He is one of the great apostles of France.

St Martin of Tours feast day is November 11th.

Question 12 ❖ Why did Saint Martin join the army?

Question 13 ❖ Of what country is Saint Martin of Tours a patron?

Question 14 ❖ To whom did Saint Martin give half his cloak?

Question 15 ❖ Who appeared to Saint Margaret Mary?

The Twelfth Station

Jesus Dies on the Cross

This Station reminds us of the most solemn moment in the history of the world – indeed, the Universe; the death of Our Lord Jesus Christ upon the Cross.

It was due to this divine act of love for us that the gates of heaven were opened which has made it possible for each one of us to be saved.
We should never cease to wonder and meditate (think) about this great event.

Jesus died on the Cross for each one of us. Yes, if you were the only person on earth, Our Lord would still have died on the Cross for you.
Jesus died on Good Friday. What a strange title for such a sad day! No, not really. It is sad that our dear Lord suffered and died, but this day was the greatest manifestation of His love for the world and the gates of heaven were opened.

It was indeed a good Friday!

Question 16 ❖ What happened on Good Friday?

Question 17 ❖ Why is it called Good Friday?

Question 18 ❖ Jesus died to make heaven possible for each one of us, but why did He do it?

Question 19 ❖ Who nailed Jesus to the Cross?

The 5th Spiritual Work of Mercy

To Bear Wrongs Patiently

This Spiritual Work of Mercy exhorts us to be patient when we are falsely accused or treated unjustly. It benefits both ourselves and our fellow man. Our patience helps him to realize his wrong doing. It is, however, wrong to permit others to falsely lay a serious crime to our charge. But let us be patient for the love of God.

Question 20 ❖ Write out the first five Spiritual Works of Mercy

Lesson 13

Level 3

Post Communion Level

Catechism

The Two Great Commandments

84. Besides believing what God has revealed, what else must we do to be saved?

Besides believing what God has revealed, we must keep His law.

85. Which are the two great commandments that contain the whole law of God?

The two great commandments that contain the whole law of God are:

first, *Thou shalt love the Lord thy God with thy whole heart, and with thy whole soul, and with thy whole mind, and with thy whole strength;*

second, *Thou shalt love thy neighbor as thyself.*

86. What must we do to love God, our neighbor, and ourselves?

To love God, our neighbor and ourselves we must keep the commandments of God and of the Church.

The ten commandments teach every man what he must do if he wants to go to heaven. In the New Testament Jesus summarized these ten commandments into two commandments. Firstly, that we should love God above all things with all our being, and the second commandment is that we should love our neighbor for the love of God. These two commandments show the virtue of charity; that is, the love of God and the love of our neighbor because of our love of God. And how do we show God we love Him? And how do we show our neighbor we love him? By keeping God's laws.

Question 1 ❖ Which are the two great commandments that contain the whole law of God?

Question 2 ❖ What virtue is shown by the keeping of the two great commandments?

Question 3 ❖ What are the rewards or punishments appointed for men after the particular judgment?

Level 3 - Lesson 13

Prayer

Hail Holy Queen

Hail, Holy Queen, Mother of Mercy, hail our life, our sweetness and our hope!
To thee do we cry, poor banished children of Eve!
To thee do we send up our sighs, mourning and weeping in this valley of tears.
Turn then, most gracious advocate, thine eyes of mercy towards us;
and after this our exile, show unto us the blessed fruit of thy womb, Jesus.
O clement, O loving, O sweet Virgin Mary!

We studied this prayer in Level Two, but prayer to Our Blessed Lady is so important, that we will revise it here. This prayer is usually said at the conclusion of the Rosary and during the prayers after low Mass. But we can pray this beautiful prayer anywhere and at any time.

The prayer is principally a prayer of petition; that is, a prayer of asking Our Lady for a share in the graces she distributes to those who ask her. Our Blessed Mother never tires of hearing our pleas for help or for graces. She desires that we ask her and she is most anxious to answer our prayers when they are said with love and confidence.

There are many prayers to Mary and the Hail, Holy Queen is indeed a beautiful one.

Question 4 ❖ When are the two times the Hail Holy Queen is usually said?

Question 5 ❖ What type of prayer is the Hail Holy Queen?

Question 6 ❖ What does Our Lady desire of us in prayer?

Question 7 ❖ What is another word for an Aspiration?

Bible Story

The Rich Man and Lazarus

Jesus told this story to his disciples: There lived once a very rich man, and he had a fine house and grounds. To the gates of this house a poor man, whose name was Lazarus. He would daily crawl to the gate as he was hungry, and covered with sores. He lay there at the gate in hopes the rich man would send him some crumbs to eat. But the rich man did not. The rich man was dressed in grand clothes, and had rich food to eat and plenty of wine to drink, but he never sent even a crumb to the poor man he knew to be at his gate. This poor man was very ill, and his sores were so bad that dogs used to come and lick him.

At length Lazarus died, and the angels came and carried him to the place of rest where Abraham is. The rich man died also, "but he was buried in hell." When he was in hell, and burning in pain and torment, he lifted his eyes, and saw this poor man with Abraham. The rich man cried out: "Father Abraham, have mercy on me, and send Lazarus that he may dip the tip of his finger in water, to cool my tongue, for I am burning in this flame." But Abraham said: "Son, thou didst receive good things in the world, food, and wine, and riches, and health, but Lazarus had not all these good things. He has now his reward and has comfort, and you have your reward in misery." Abraham told him besides that none could go from heaven to hell, or from hell to heaven.

Jesus had told His disciples many things, but there was yet a great deal for them to know. He had made Peter head of His disciples, because Peter had strong faith, and had said that Jesus was "the Son of the living God." He also told them that soon He would be put to a cruel death, and that He should be delivered up into the hands of His enemies.

Question 8	❖	What happens to us if we live a life of selfishness and greed, not caring about others.?
Question 9	❖	What was the name of the poor man who lived at the gate of the rich man, hoping for a little food?
Question 10	❖	Who does the father in the story of the Prodigal Son represent?

The Saints

Saint Teresa of Avila

There were two great Saint Teresa's. One is called the Little Flower. The other is called the Great Saint Teresa. She was the Holy Mother of the Carmelite Sisters. The Little Flower was one of her lovely spiritual children. When the Great Saint Teresa was a little girl, she ran away from home with her brother, because she wanted to die as a Matyr. Her unlce found her quickly and bought her back to her parents' house. Later she became a sister. She grieved for all the sinners in the world who did not love God "I will love Him all the harder because they do not," she said.

"Dear God," she prayed, "forgive them. See! I will suffer and do penance for their sins." So she slept on hard boards. She never ate meat. She prayed for long hours. She said to God, "Please let me love You. Please let me suffer for their sins. And do not punish the people who hate You and who are wicked." Many holy young women joined her. They prayed for sinners. They asked God to keep young people from temptation. They loved God like dear daughters. The Great Saint Teresa built convents for them all over the world. They are the Carmelite Nuns.

Saint Teresa of Avila Feast day is October 15th

Question 11 ❖ What is Saint Teresa of Avila sometimes called?

Question 12 ❖ What Religious Order was Saint Teresa the Mother?

Question 13 ❖ Which country is Saint Martin of Tours a patron?

The Thirteenth Station

Jesus is Taken Down From the Cross

After Our Lord's suffering and death, His sacred Body was taken down from the Cross by Joseph of Arimathea and Nicodemus, (two holy disciples of Jesus) and placed into the arms of holy Mary.

Our Lord's suffering was complete but His blessed Mother was still suffering as she held her Son's dead body in her arms.

A famous artist, Michael Angelo sculptured this sad scene in a famous piece of art called the Pieta. The statue is in Saint Peter's Basilica in Rome. When we think about this Station of the Cross, we think about the love which Mary has for each one of us. She witnessed her Son's suffering and death, and suffered with Him.

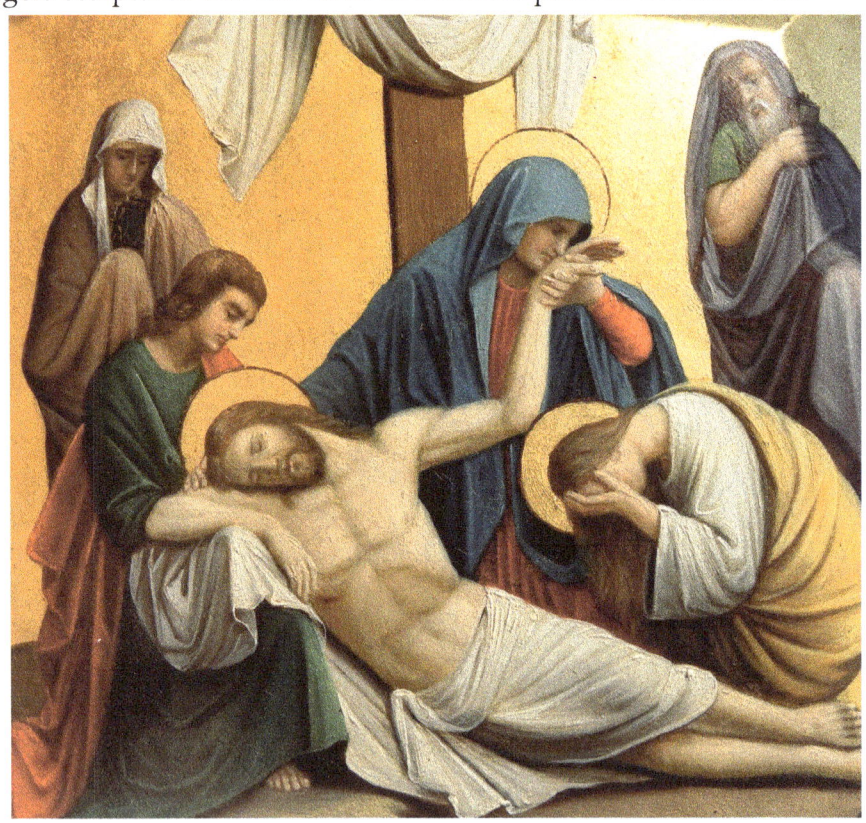

Let us pray to her and ask for strength when we have things to suffer.

Question 15 ❖ What was the name of the famous artwork by Michael Angelo?

Question 16 ❖ Who were the two disciples who took Jesus down from the Cross?

Question 17 ❖ Into whose arms was Jesus placed?

Question 18 ❖ Why is it called Good Friday?

The 6th Spiritual Work of Mercy

To Forgive all Injuries

When Our Lord was raised on the Cross, with men mocking Him, spitting on Him and blaspheming, He simply said, Father, forgive them, for they know not what they do.

Are we so ready to forgive our enemies or those who are hurting us? Jesus has given us the example and we must follow.

This is a very difficult Work of Mercy for many people, because we have to fight against ourselves. To love one's enemies is not natural. It is supernatural! Therefore, we must not seek revenge, but we must imitate Our Lord and the Saints and pray and even help those who have injured us.
Yes, this is a spiritual work of mercy that we need to ask God's help for.

Question 19 ❖ What did Jesus say about His enemies while hanging on the Cross?

Question 20 ❖ Why is the sixth Spiritual Work of Mercy so difficult?

Question 21 ❖ Write out the first six Spiritual Works of Mercy.

Lesson 14

Level 3

Post Communion Level

Catechism

The Ten Commandments

87.   **Which are the commandments of God?**

The commandments of God are these ten:
1. *I am the Lord thy God; thou shalt not have strange Gods before Me.*
2. *Thou shalt not take the name of the Lord thy God in vain.*
3. *Remember thou keep holy the Lord's day.*
4. *Honor thy father and thy mother.*
5. *Thou shalt not kill.*
6. *Thou shalt not commit adultery.*
7. *Thou shalt not steal.*
8. *Thou shalt not bear false witness against thy neighbor.*
9. *Thou shalt not covet thy neighbor's wife.*
10. *Thou shalt not covet thy neighbor's goods.*

This lesson's catechism question is simply the Ten Commandments. We have studied in some detail these commandments in Lesson 6. It is very important that they be learnt by heart.

After Moses had freed the Israelites from Egypt, God took him up to the top of Mount Sinai and gave him the Ten Commandments on two tablets of stone. On the first tablet were the first three commandments which concern our duties towards God. On the second tablet are the last seven commandments concerning our duties towards our neighbor.

Question 1 ❖ To whom did God give the Ten Commandments?

Question 2 ❖ How many Commandments are there and on how many tablets of stone were they given?

Question 3 ❖ Upon which tablet of stone were the commandments concerning our duties towards God?

Level 3 - Lesson 14

Prayer

Anima Christi

Soul of Christ, sanctify me.
Body of Christ, save me.
Blood of Christ, inebriate me.
Water from the side of Christ, wash me.
Passion of Christ, strengthen me.
O good Jesus, hear me.
Within Thy wounds, hide me.
Suffer me not to be separated from Thee.
From the malicious enemy defend me.
In the hour of my death, call me.
And bid me come unto Thee.
That with Thy saints I may praise Thee.
For ever and ever. Amen.

This is a beautiful prayer (called in English, Soul of Christ) which is best said at Mass after having received Holy Communion.

At this Level, you do not have to learn it by heart, although it is recommended that you do so.

This is a prayer that should be said slowly and quietly, by yourself, while meditating (thinking about) upon the words you are saying.

This prayer is begging God to make you holy. Thus you see, what a wonderful prayer it is: a prayer for holiness.

Question 4 ❖ When is the Anima Christi best said?

Question 5 ❖ What does Anima Christi mean?

Question 6 ❖ What type of prayer is Anima Christi and what are we asking for?

Bible Story

Jesus Raises Lazarus From the Dead

In a village called Bethany, lived another Lazarus, with his two sisters. Martha and Mary. Jesus loved this family very much, and often went to visit them. One day Martha and Mary sent word to Jesus that Lazarus, his friend, was very ill. When the messenger told Our Lord, Jesus said: "Lazarus is sick only that the glory of God and My power may be shown in him." Jesus was staying then in the country ; and two days after He had been told that Lazarus was so ill, He called His disciples and said to them: "Lazarus our friend is asleep, and we must go to Bethany and wake him up." But His disciples said: "Lord, if he sleep he shall do well." But Jesus meant that Lazarus was dead. So He said to them plainly: "Lazarus is dead, and I am glad for your sakes that I was not there, that you may believe: but let us go to him." When they arrived at Bethany, Lazarus had been dead four days, and in his grave.

In those countries people are buried the day they die. Martha, when she heard Jesus had come, went to see Him, and said to Him: "Lord, if Thou hadst been here my brother had not died; but I know that whatever Thou wilt ask of God, He will give it Thee." Now Mary was in the house with friends and many Jews who came to mourn with them. Martha went and told Mary: "The Master is come and calleth for thee." When Mary heard that Jesus asked for her, she rose with haste, left her friends, and went to Jesus. Falling down at His feet, she said: "Lord, if Thou hadst been here, my brother had not died." Jesus, when He saw her tears, and the Jews who had followed her weeping also, was very sorry for her, and He was full of trouble. He asked: "Where have you laid (buried) him?" And they said to Him: "Lord, come and see." "And Jesus wept." The Jews, therefore, said: "Behold, how He loved him." But some of them said: "Could not He that opened the eyes of the man born blind, have caused that this man should not die?"

Jesus, when He came to the grave, over which there was a stoned placed, directed them to "take away the stone." Martha, when she heard this, did not like to have it moved, and said to Jesus: "Lord, by this time he smells, for he is now buried four days." But Jesus told her to have faith, and she would see the power of God. So the stone was rolled away. Jesus then gave thanks to God, and cried out with a loud voice: "Lazarus , come forth!" At once, just as he was, all wrapped in cloths, out came Lazarus from his grave, and Jesus told them to untie the cloths.

What joy it must have been to Martha and Mary, and how glad Jesus must have felt to see the joy of these friends! For Jesus likes to make people happy. This was, indeed, a great wonder, and all those who had seen it went about the country and to Jerusalem telling how Lazarus, who was four days dead, was brought to life again by Jesus. When the Jews and those wicked people who had power in Jerusalem heard of it they were jealous of Jesus and hated Him. They made up their minds that the first chance they had they would kill Him.

Bible Story

Question 7 ❖ Why did Jesus not cure Lazarus when told he was sick?

Question 8 ❖ What made the Jews say, "Behold, how He loved him"?

Question 9 ❖ What was this great miracle?

Question 10 ❖ What did those wicked Jews want to do after hearing of this great miracle?

Question 11 ❖ What was the name of the poor man who lived at the gate of the rich man, hoping for a little food?

The Saints

Saint Louis IX

Louis was a fine, strong, pure boy. His mother taught him to hate sin. Her name was Blanche. "I love you, my son," she said, "but I would rather see you dead than have you commit one mortal sin." He remembered this all his life. He was made King of France. He determined to be a good and generous king. Each day he found time to hear two Masses. He prayed far into the night.

In those days, the Mohammedans hated Christians. They were trying to destroy the Christian countries. They had great armies. They sailed powerful fleets. It looked as if they would win. But Louis made sure they would not. He gathered a great army and marched out to fight them. He was so brave and fine that the Mohammedans respected him. Some of them asked him to be their king. Yet God did not wish him to win with the sword. He really seemed to lose that war. Only he didn't. The Mohammedans never conquered the Christian lands.

Saint Louis IX Feast day is August 25th.

Question 12 ❖ Of what country was Louis IX king?

Question 13 ❖ What was the name of Louis IX's mother?

Question 14 ❖ What did King Louis IX do twice every day?

The Fourteenth Station

Jesus is Laid in the Sepulchre

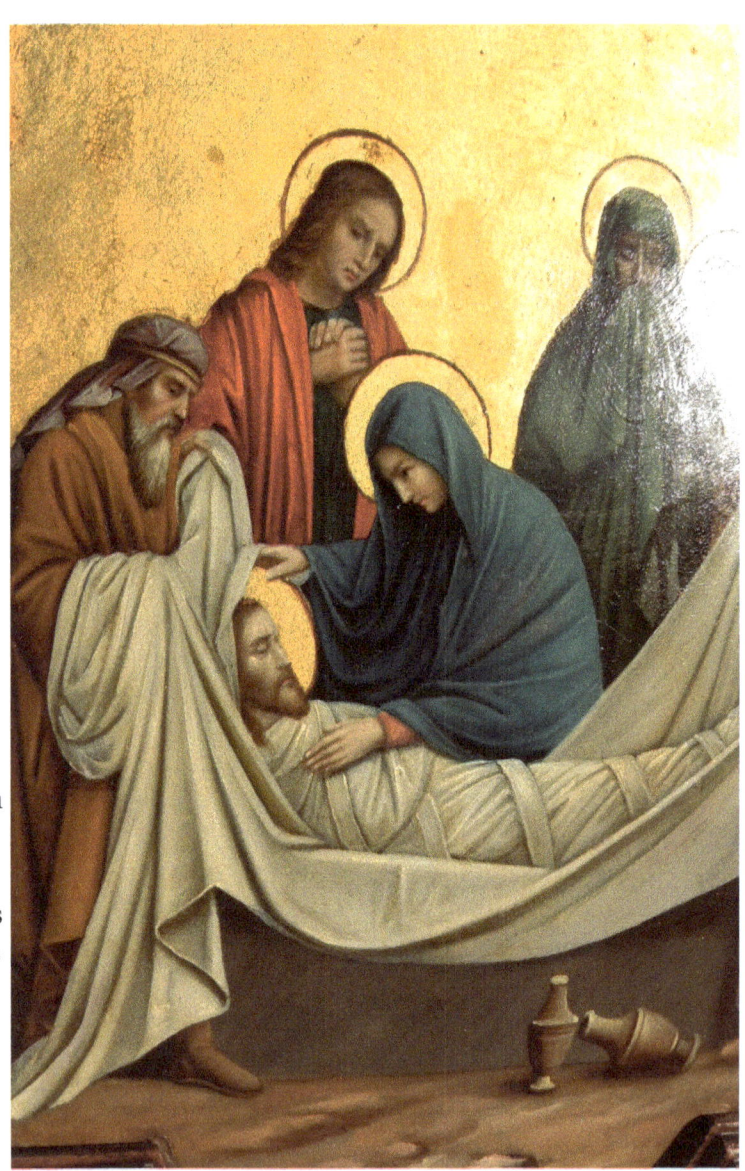

After being taken down from the Cross and placed into the arms of His Holy Mother, Jesus was taken and wrapped in a shroud and carefully and lovingly placed in the tomb prepared for Saint Joseph of Arimathea.

This was done before 6:00pm on Friday and Jesus remained in the sepulchre (tomb) until just after midnight on Easter Sunday morning.

While the body of Jesus lay in the tomb, his soul went to the Limbo of the Fathers (where the good people of the Old Testament were waiting for the gates of heaven to be opened). Jesus brought them the news of His death and told them that the gates of heaven were now unlocked and they could follow Him shortly into heaven.

Many people (even some of the followers of Jesus) thought this was the end of Him, but we know it was only the beginning. For on Easter Sunday, Our Lord rose gloriously from the dead.

Question 15 ❖ What does the word sepulchre mean?

Question 16 ❖ Where did the soul of Jesus go while His body was in the tomb?

Question 17 ❖ Jesus was buried in whose tomb?

Question 18 ❖ List the fourteen Stations of the Cross in order.

Level 3 - Lesson 14

The 7th Spiritual Work of Mercy

To Pray for the Living and the Dead

We may not see the effects of our prayers, but God sees them. Not one single prayer raised to God from a sincere heart is wasted. "More things are wrought by prayer than this world dreams of." Prayers do good not only to those we pray for, but to ourselves.

When we pray, we pray for both the living and the dead. We pray that those living will avoid mortal sin and save their souls, and for the dead who might be in Purgatory, we pray that their sufferings will soon come to an end and they will enter the glory of heaven.

Question 19 ❖ Write out the seven Spiritual Works of Mercy.

Question 20 ❖ Why do we pray for the dead?

Lesson 15

Level 3

Post Communion Level

Catechism

This is the last lesson of the year and is different to all other lessons. It is a summary of all you have learned this year.

A summary important as it gives you the opportunity to review all the things you have already studied, so that you have a better knowledge of your work and you will therefore be more pleasing to God.

Catechism Questions :

46. **What is meant by the Redemption?**
    By the Redemption is meant that Jesus Christ offered His sufferings and death to God in satisfaction for the sins of men.

47. **What do we learn from the sufferings and death of Christ?**
    From the sufferings and death of Christ we learn God's love for man and the evil of sin.

48. **What do we mean when we say in the Apostles' Creed that Christ descended into hell?**
    When we say that Christ descended into hell we mean that, after He died the soul of Christ descended into a place or state of rest, called limbo, where the souls of the just were waiting for Him.

49. **When did Christ rise from the dead?**
    Christ rose from the dead, glorious and immortal, on Easter Sunday, the third day after His death.

50. **When did Christ ascend into heaven?**
    Christ ascended, body and soul, into heaven on Ascension Day, forty days after His Resurrection.

51. **What do we mean when we say that Christ sits at the right hand of God, the Father Almighty?**
    When we say that Christ sits at the right hand of God, the Father Almighty, we mean that Our Lord as God is equal to the Father, and that as man He has the highest place in heaven, next to God.

Catechism

52. **What do we mean when we say that Christ will come from thence to judge the living and the dead?**
When we say that Christ will come from thence to judge the living and the dead, we mean that on the last day Our Lord will come to judge everyone who has ever lived in this world.

53. **Who is the Holy Ghost?**
The Holy Ghost is God and the third Person of the Blessed Trinity.

54. **What does the Holy Ghost do for the salvation of mankind?**
The Holy Ghost sanctifies souls through the gift of grace.

55. **How many kinds of grace are there?**
There are two kinds of grace: sanctifying grace and actual grace.

56. **What does sanctifying grace do for us?**
Sanctifying grace:
first, *makes us holy and pleasing to God;*
second, *makes us adopted children of God;*
third, *makes us temples of the Holy Ghost;*
fourth, *gives us the right to heaven.*

57. **What is actual grace?**
Actual grace is a supernatural help of God which enlightens our mind and strengthens our will to do good and to avoid evil.

58. **What are the principal ways of obtaining grace?**
The principal ways of obtaining grace are prayer and the sacraments, especially the Holy Eucharist.

59. **What are the chief powers that are given to us with sanctifying grace?**
The chief powers that are given to us with sanctifying grace are the three theological virtues and the seven gifts of the Holy Ghost.

60. **What are the three theological virtues?**
The three theological virtues are faith, hope and charity.

Catechism

61. What is faith?
Faith is the virtue by which we firmly believe in the word of God all the truths He has revealed.

62. What is hope?
Hope is the virtue by which we firmly trust that God will give us eternal happiness and the means to obtain it.

63. What is Charity?
Charity is the virtue by which we love God above all things for His own sake, and our neighbor as ourselves.

64. Which are the seven gifts of the Holy Ghost?
The seven gifts of the Holy Ghost are: wisdom, understanding, counsel, fortitude, knowledge, piety and fear of the Lord.

65. What is the Church?
The Church is the congregation of all baptized persons united in the same true faith, the same sacrifice, and the same sacraments, under the Holy Father, the Pope.

66. Why did Jesus Christ found the Church?
Jesus Christ founded the Church to bring all men to eternal salvation.

67. To whom did Christ give the power to teach, to sanctify and to rule the members of His Church?
Christ gave the power to teach, to sanctify, and to rule the members of His Church to the apostles, the first bishops of the Church.

68. Who are the successors of the apostles?
The successors of the apostles are the bishops of the Church.

69. Did Christ give special power in His Church to any one of the apostles?
Christ gave special power in His Church to Saint Peter by making him the head of the apostles and the chief teacher and ruler of the entire Church.

Catechism

70. **Who is the successor of Saint Peter?**
    The successor of Saint Peter is the Holy Father, the Bishop of Rome.

71. **Who helps the bishops in the care of souls?**
    The priests, especially parish priests, help the bishops in the care of souls.

72. **Which is the one true Church established by Christ?**
    The one true Church established by Christ is the Catholic Church.

73. **How do we know that the Catholic Church is the one true Church established by Christ?**
    We know that the Catholic Church is the one true Church established by Christ because it alone has the marks of the true Church.

74. **What are the chief marks of the Church?**
    The chief marks of the Church are four: It is one, holy, catholic or universal, and apostolic.

75. **Are all obliged to belong to the Catholic Church in order to be saved?**
    All are obliged to belong to the Catholic Church, in some way, in order to be saved.

76. **What is meant by "the communion of saints" in the Apostles' Creed?**
    By "the communion of saints" is meant the union of the faithful on earth, the blessed in heaven, and the souls in purgatory, with Christ as their Head.

77. **What is meant in the Apostles' Creed by "the forgiveness of sins"?**
    By "the forgiveness of sins" in the Apostles' Creed is meant that God has given to the Church, through Jesus Christ, the power to forgive sins.

78. **What is meant by "the resurrection of the body"?**
    By "the resurrection of the body" is meant that at the end of the world the bodies of all men will rise from the earth and be united again to their souls, nevermore to be separated.

79. **Has the body of any human person ever been taken into heaven?**
    By the special favor of her Assumption, the body of the Blessed Virgin Mary was raised from the dead and taken into heaven.

Catechism

80. **What is the judgment called which will be passed on all men immediately after the general resurrection?**
The judgment which will be passed on each one of us immediately after death is called the particular judgment.

81. **What is the judgment called which will be passed on each one of us immediately after death?**
The judgment which will be passed on all men immediately after the general resurrection is called the general judgment.

82. **What are the rewards or punishments appointed for men after the particular judgment?**
The rewards or punishments appointed for men after the particular judgment are heaven, purgatory, or hell.

83. **What is meant by the word "Amen" with which we end the Apostles' Creed?**
By the word "Amen," with which we end the Apostles' Creed, is meant "So it is," or "So be it."

84. **Besides believing what God has revealed, what else must we do to be saved?**
Besides believing what God has revealed, we must keep His law.

85. **Which are the two great commandments that contain the whole law of God?**
The two great commandments that contain the whole law of God are:
first, *Thou shalt love the Lord thy God with thy whole heart, and with thy whole soul, and with thy whole mind, and with thy whole strength;*
second, *Thou shalt love thy neighbor as thyself.*

86. **What must we do to love God, our neighbor, and ourselves?**
To love God, our neighbor, and ourselves we must keep the commandments of God and of the Church.

Catechism

87. Which are the commandments of God?

The commandments of God are these ten:

1. *I am the Lord thy God; thou shalt not have strange Gods before Me.*

2. *Thou shalt not take the name of the Lord thy God in vain.*

3. *Remember thou keep holy the Lord's day.*

4. *Honor thy father and thy mother.*

5. *Thou shalt not kill.*

6. *Thou shalt not commit adultery.*

7. *Thou shalt not steal.*

8. *Thou shalt not bear false witness against thy neighbor.*

9. *Thou shalt not covet thy neighbor's wife.*

10. *Thou shalt not covet thy neighbor's goods.*

www.ingramcontent.com/pod-product-compliance
Lightning Source LLC
Chambersburg PA
CBHW061749290426
44108CB00028B/2930